FAMOUS
FASHION
DESIGNERS

COCO CHANEL

FAMOUS
FASHION
DESIGNERS

COCO CHANEL

MARC JACOBS

CALVIN KLEIN

RALPH LAUREN

STELLA McCARTNEY

ISAAC MIZRAHI

VALENTINO

VERSACE

FAMOUS
FASHION
DESIGNERS

COCO CHANEL

Dennis Abrams

CHELSEA HOUSE
An Infobase Learning Company

COCO CHANEL

Copyright © 2011 by Infobase Learning

Chelsea House
An imprint of Infobase Learning
132 West 31st Street
New York NY 10001

Library of Congress Cataloging-in-Publication Data

Abrams, Dennis, 1960-
    Coco Chanel / by Dennis Abrams.
        p. cm. — (Famous fashion designers)
    Includes bibliographical references and index.
    ISBN 978-1-60413-925-9 (hardcover)
    1. Chanel, Coco, 1883-1971—Juvenile literature. 2. Fashion designers—France—Biography—Juvenile literature. 3. Women fashion designers—France—Biography—Juvenile literature. I. Chanel, Coco, 1883-1971. II. Title.
    TT505.C45A27 2011
    746.9'2092—dc22
    [B]   2010034100

Chelsea House books are available at special discounts when purchased in bulk quantities for businesses, associations, institutions, or sales promotions. Please call our Special Sales Department in New York at (212) 967-8800 or (800) 322-8755.

You can find Chelsea House on the World Wide Web at
http://www.chelseahouse.com

Text design and composition by Lina Farinella
Cover design by Alicia Post
Cover printed by Yurchak Printing, Landisville, Pa.
Book printed and bound by Yurchak Printing, Landisville, Pa.
Printed in the United States of America

Contents

1

The Comeback

The date was February 5, 1954, chosen for the good luck that the number 5 had always brought her. Fashion designer Gabrielle Chanel, known to the world as Coco, was the head of one of the greatest fashion empires in the world. But it had been 25 years since she had presented the world with a new line in fashion. It was time for her to make a comeback.

She had a lot to live up to. During her active years as a designer, she had completely redefined women's fashion. She removed women from the tight, constraining corsets and stays of an earlier age and dressed them in slimmed down, almost masculine clothing that liberated them both physically and emotionally.

She dressed women in blazers and in straight skirts. She produced beaded dresses. She created the two- and three-piece women's suit, known forever as the Chanel suit. She pioneered the

After introducing her new collection following years of retirement, Gabrielle "Coco" Chanel relaxes in her book-lined studio above her Paris salon on April 21, 1954.

little black dress that is to this day found in the closet of every well-dressed woman. She introduced costume jewelry to the world. She gave the world its most popular and best-known perfume, Chanel No. 5. She established simple daytime ensembles of dresses and coats. In fact, the entire concept of women's sportswear, of clothes that allow women to move, came directly from Chanel's boutique on rue Cambon in Paris.

But she did more than give the world of women's clothing a whole new look. She gave the world herself as well. She became an icon, an example of a woman who came from nothing and yet still managed to establish herself as a world-famous designer and businesswoman. Her every move was news. She was photographed and sought after by the highest levels of society. Hollywood wanted her to design clothing for films. She became more than just a fashion designer. She became Coco Chanel.

But all that had been in the past. With the outbreak of World War II in 1939, the very notion of introducing an annual collection of high-fashion clothing went out the window. And then years later, in the aftermath of the war, Chanel found herself living a quiet life of semiretirement in Switzerland. Eventually, though, her need to design, to produce new clothes and to be number one became too much for her. She returned to Paris in 1953, ready to assume her position as the world's preeminent designer.

The fashion landscape had dramatically changed while she was away, however. In 1947, designer Christian Dior had stunned the world with what became known as the New Look. Gone were the restrained, streamlined clothes of the war and its aftermath. In their place was clothing that once again emphasized the woman's bustline and cinched in tight at the waist. And, to flaunt the wartime restrictions on the use of fabric, yard after yard of rich fabrics were used in his creations—sometimes as much as 20 yards (18.3 meters) of material.

This was clothing, not simple and timeless as Chanel saw it, but clothing as statement, clothing as costume, clothing as art. In a world eager to throw off the traumas of World War II, it was a look that struck an immediate chord with fashion-hungry Parisians. "Women had been deprived of everything for five years so they threw themselves on fashion like hungry beasts," Marquise Emmita de la Falaise later recalled, as quoted in Axel Madsen's *Chanel: A Woman of Her Own.*

Other designers such as Hubert de Givenchy, Pierre Balmain, and Pierre Cardin soon entered the arena. The world of French high fashion, once dominated by women such as Gabrielle Chanel, Elsa Schiaparelli, and Nina Ricci, was now being dominated by men. As she prepared for her 1954 show, the world had just one question: Would Chanel be able to change with the times?

THE 1954 SHOW

She was 70 years old and thin, with a wide mouth, sharp jaw, strongly penciled-in eyebrows, and strong hands and fingers free from nail polish. With the exception of the enormous glasses she now sometimes needed, Chanel looked much the same as she did in 1939 when she had shut down the House of Chanel for the duration of the war.

One other thing that remained the same was her determination. Her confidence and her undying belief that while other fashion trends may come and go, her line would forever remain a classic kept her going. She remained convinced that fashion should not be a "new look" that changes annually, but a look that was flattering to women but not overwhelming; one that was easy to wear and would remain timeless regardless of other fashion trends. To Chanel, a dress was not a costume or a disguise. To her, if a fashion was not something that could be adapted and worn by everybody, it was not fashion—it was simply an affectation, a fancy dress.

A Place to Display Her Clothes

In 1928, at the near peak of her success, Gabrielle Chanel expanded her business, which had started at 25, rue Cambon, to include numbers 27, 29, and 31, which the House of Chanel rents to this day.

It was there that she installed glass mirrors and simple chandeliers in her couture salon. These faceted mirrors, which created the Modernist impression of endless space, of a wall-less room expanding into infinity, is where Chanel presented her latest collections. Chanel herself sat safely where the audience couldn't see her, at the top of the stairs where she had an eagle-eye perspective on both her models and the reaction of the crowd.

She went to work with a vengeance, ready to reclaim her crown. She worked long hours on each piece of clothing, pulling them apart and putting them back together, shortening the hems, lengthening the hems, doing everything in her power to refine her look while still retaining its fundamental lines.

She began speaking to the press, giving "exclusive" interviews to every reporter who would listen. She told interviewers, as quoted by Axel Madsen, that she had told her rival Dior, "I adore you, but you dress women like armchairs." When asked what her new line would look like, she snapped, "How do I know? I keep changing until the last moment."

One thing she did promise interviewers, though, was that, as always, her clothes would be designed to make a woman look pretty. She would not, as so many of the new designers seemed to be doing, be designing beautiful clothes without considering how they actually made the woman look and feel. According to Amy De La Haye and Shelley Tobin in *Chanel: The Couturiere at Work,* Chanel believed

> a dress isn't right if it is uncomfortable. Nothing shows age more than the upper arms, cover them. Buttons must have button-holes, pockets be in the right place, usable. A sleeve isn't right unless the arm lifts easily. Elegance in fashion means freedom to move freely.

On the evening before the premiere, Chanel was still hard at work. She had the models walk in front of her while she lay flat on her stomach, to make absolutely certain that the hems were right. She had boxes of flowers, ribbons, and other additions, ready to be added if necessary. But instead, as was usually the case, she more often removed details from the designs rather than added them. Her fashion was always a paring down.

The show was scheduled for 2:00 P.M. and was considered the hottest fashion show in Paris that season. Held in Chanel's own salon, the room was filled 30 minutes before the show began,

Coco Chanel sits on the stairs overlooking her Paris showroom and watches her "comeback" show.

ELEMENTS OF STYLE

Fashion is at once both caterpillar and butterfly. Be a caterpillar by day and a butterfly by night. Nothing could be more comfortable than a caterpillar and nothing more made for love than a butterfly. There must be dresses that crawl and dresses that fly. The butterfly does not go to market, and the caterpillar does not go to a ball.

—*from* Chanel and Her World: Friends, Fashion, and Fame

by Edmonde Charles-Roux

with crowds of "beautiful people," fashion buyers, members of the press, and photographers.

When the show began, Coco Chanel was nowhere to be seen. She was in her usual perch, at the top of a mirrored staircase to the side of the runway, which gave her the ideal angle to see how her fashions looked on the models as they moved, as well as the reaction of the audience. The crowd held their collective breath as the show began.

What followed, as each model entered, posed, paused long enough for the fashion editors to feel the fabric of the clothing, posed again, and then turned and exited, was stunned silence. Much to the crowd's shock and amazement, despite all of the changes in the world of fashion since 1939, despite all of the changes in the world since 1939, Chanel's look hadn't changed. Instead of a new Chanel look, there remained "the look," a look of simplicity, one constantly refined over the years, but essentially unchanged.

The reviews that appeared in the papers the next day were disastrous. Lucien François, the fashion "oracle" from *Le Combat*, opened with the headline "Chez Coco Chanel à Fouilly-Les-Oies en 1930" (roughly, "In the Sticks with 1930 Coco Chanel"), quoted in Axel Madsen's biography: "From the first dress we knew that the Chanel style belonged to the past. Dresses tucked in at the waist, balloon sleeves, round décolleté conjured up little more than a furtive memory of a period that is hard to situate, 1929–30, no doubt. Chanel makes herself so much at home in a legend idealized by memories that we forget her fashion was already mortally wounded in 1938. But there are no 1938 dresses here, only ghosts of 1930!"

The leading French newspaper, *Le Figaro*, joined the chorus of naysayers, noting snidely (as cited by Madsen) that "it was touching. You had a feeling you were back in 1925." The reviews from London were no better. The *Daily Express* headlined its story "A Fiasco—Audience Gasped!" before pointing out that it seemed too soon to try and recapture the look of the prewar era. Another London critic called it a collection fit for mothers. They were the worst reviews of Chanel's long and illustrious career.

France's leading afternoon newspaper, *France-Soir*, got Chanel's reaction, as quoted by Madsen: "What can I tell you? People no longer know what elegance is. When I work, I think of the women I try to dress, not the couture house. How can anyone get it so wrong? Once I helped liberate women. I'll do it again."

COULD SHE?

The question still remained: Could the now 71-year-old Gabrielle "Coco" Chanel remain relevant in a fashion world seemingly geared to what was going to be the "next big thing"? To many, it seemed that she was a forgotten relic of the past, a designer whose time had come and long since gone.

But to anyone who knew her well, the chances that she would let bad reviews stop her seemed highly unlikely. She was a woman driven to succeed, constantly striving to be the best. She was a woman so determined to succeed that, against all odds, she had risen from a poverty-stricken background to dress some of the world's wealthiest women. A woman so determined to rise to the top that she cut herself off from her own past, presenting the world with an image and a life that bore little resemblance to where she had actually come from. She was Coco Chanel. She had made it to the top once. If talent and drive had anything to with it, she would do so again.

2

Childhood:
Fact and Myth

*At the age of six, I am already alone. My mother has just died.
My father deposits me, like a millstone, at the house of my
aunts, and leaves immediately for an America from which he
will never return. An orphan . . . ever since then, this word has
paralyzed me with fear; even now I cannot go past a girls'
boarding school and hear people say "they are orphans,"
without tears coming to my eyes.*

(Coco Chanel to Paul Morand, *The Allure of Chanel*)

At the end of World War II, Gabrielle Chanel, in exile in
Switzerland, sat down with Paul Morand, a diplomat,
writer, and socialite, for a series of interviews that she
hoped would become her memoirs. The memoir never came to be.
And, given the above example, that is probably for the best. For virtually nothing in that "memory" from Chanel's childhood is true.

Her father was 27-year-old Albert Chanel, a traveling merchant who dealt in wine, bonnets, buttons, overalls, and kitchen aprons. Her mother was 19-year-old Jeanne Devolle. The couple was not married. In fact, Devolle was already the mother of another child, named Julie.

Julie had been born on September 11, 1882, and although Albert acknowledged that he was the father, he refused to marry Jeanne, who nonetheless left her hometown of Courpière and accompanied Albert to the garrison town of Saumur. It was there, just three months after the birth of Julie, that Jeanne became pregnant again. And it was in a poorhouse hospice that Gabrielle was born on August 19, 1883. Albert Chanel was nowhere to be seen.

MARRIAGE AND DEATH

But one year later, on November 17, 1884, Albert Chanel and Eugénie Jeanne Devolle were married. Jeanne brought to the marriage a dowry of 5,000 francs, along with furniture and personal items worth an additional 500 francs. In return, Albert legalized his paternity of Julie and Gabrielle.

Marriage did not change their lives. Albert continued his life as a migrant market merchant, traveling from town to town, from local market to local market, setting up a small stand and selling his goods. More children were born. A son, Alphonse, in 1885. Another daughter, Antoinette, destined to become Gabrielle's favorite, in 1887.

With four children in tow, Jeanne moved back to her hometown to live with her uncle Augustin. According to biographer Axel Madsen, it was perhaps the best time of the children's childhoods. Jeanne, afraid that Albert might never return, often went out on the road with her husband, leaving the children to be looked after by her large extended family.

The oldest child, Julie, grew up, as described by Axel Madsen, as "slow-witted and afraid of everything," so Gabrielle spent much of her time playing with her brother, Alphonse. But just as often,

Gabrielle Chanel was born into poverty in the town of Saumur, France (*above*).

she was playing by herself. Indeed, some of her earliest memories were of playing alone in an old churchyard cemetery, surrounded by weed-covered graves. In her mind, it was her own secret garden, her own hideaway, where she was the queen and defender of all who resided there. "I told myself that the dead are not really dead as long as people think about them," she is quoted as saying years later by Madsen.

It was a childhood story she told and retold throughout her life. In some versions, she said her family tried to lure her away from the cemetery by telling her that none of her *own* family was buried there. In Madsen's *Chanel: A Woman of Her Own*, she is quoted as saying:

That didn't bother me. I brought flowers, and forks and spoons and whatever else I could steal from home, and spread out my loot around the graves. One day, my family discovered the stuff that was missing. They locked everything up and since I could no longer bring things to my dead, I forgot about them.

Yet in other variations, she said she brought her rag dolls to the cemetery. And in the version she related to Paul Morand, she explained she spoke to the dead because she felt she had nobody to talk to at home.

I wanted to be sure that I was loved, but I lived with people who showed no pity. I like talking to myself and I don't listen to what I'm told: this is probably due to the fact that the first people to whom I opened my heart were the dead.

(Paul Morand, *The Allure of Chanel*)

And many, many years later, when she was a very old and sometimes lonely woman, Gabrielle Chanel was again often found in cemeteries, talking quietly to her dead.

ABANDONMENT

In 1889, already the mother of children ages seven, six, four, and two, Jeanne Chanel gave birth to another son, Lucien, in a tavern at the market town of Guéret. Soon, Jeanne Chanel's life of poverty, constant travel, and frequent pregnancies (another son named Augustin had been born, and another, Coupiere, had died in infancy) had destroyed her health. In February 1895, she was found dead in a freezing cold room in the market town of Brive-la-Gaillarde, her husband away again on the road. She was just 32 years old. Gabrielle Chanel was 11. And with her mother's death, she was now truly alone.

With Jeanne's death, Albert Chanel disappeared for good. Julie, Gabrielle, and Antoinette Chanel, in large part, would spend the next six years at an orphanage called Aubazine, run by the sisters of the Congregation of the Sacred Heart. Her brothers, Alphonse and Lucien, were sent to live with farmers, where they worked unpaid as virtual slaves from the age of eight.

AUBAZINE

High on a plateau above the Corrèze River, the orphanage was, in a word, bleak. Sitting among the monastery's former abbey and the ruins of a medieval cloister, it had a steep roof, high walls, and an enclosed courtyard. The orphans wore simple, white blouses and black skirts. The walls and corridors were painted white; the doors to the dormitories were painted black.

The girls were divided into two groups: those whose family could pay something to the nuns, and those, like the Chanel girls, who could not. So even though Chanel continued to insist to her fellow orphans that her father did send money and was going to come back for her after he made his fortune in America, the Chanel girls, along with the other destitute children, were forced to sleep in an unheated dormitory and to eat their meals apart from the others.

What Aubazine did provide, though, thanks to French government reforms dating back to 1870, was an education. It wasn't the most thorough of educations, but six days a week, Gabrielle Chanel attended classes and learned the basics of reading, writing, geography, and history.

There was not a lot of free time. After classes and studying, evenings were spent performing household tasks; specifically, learning to sew by hemming sheets and knitting baby clothes. Sunday mornings, not surprisingly, were spent at Mass, but often on Sunday afternoons, one of the teachers would take the girls on an outing outside of the walls of Aubazine and on a hike to the summit of Le Coiroux.

But although Chanel never made reference to her years at Aubazine, its impact was with her for the remainder of her life. The simple life, the simple clothes, the austerity of her life there

Women Under Constraint

The well-dressed woman of the late nineteenth century was under constraints in many ways. Women had few legal rights, were unable to vote, and lacked the educational and career opportunities that were open to men.

They were constrained by their clothing as well. The fashion of the day dictated that the well-dressed woman lace herself into a corset, a tight-fitting undergarment with rigid vertical boning and a mold that bound her stomach and waist, pushing the hips backward while at the same time pushing up and emphasizing her bustline. Corsets were tight and uncomfortable, and they made it difficult for women to move freely, but men appreciated the curves they gave to a woman's body.

But as the early twentieth century progressed, the time had come for a change. Women had become more active, and during World War I they were forced to go to work in large numbers. Chanel recognized this and, in her fashion, released women from the constraints of the corset, saying, "To the woman going to work I said to take off the bone corset, because women cannot work while they're imprisoned in a corset."

For this moment of liberation, generations of women have been eternally grateful.

made a lasting impression. Edmonde Charles-Roux, an editor of French *Vogue* who wrote a biography of Chanel, speculated on the meaning of those years.

> Whenever she began yearning for austerity, for the ultimate in cleanliness, for faces scrubbed with yellow soap; or waxed nostalgic for all things white, simple, and clean, for linen piled in high cupboards, white-washed walls, . . . one had to understand that she was speaking in a secret code, and that every word she uttered meant only one word, Aubazine.

Even so, Aubazine was not the place she felt that she should be. She strongly felt that she was different from the others, and she resisted orders, saying "no" to anything and everything she could. She hated the solemnities of Mass, hated having to kneel, hated having to bow her head. "I was a pest, a thief, someone who listens at doors," she told Morand in 1946. "I hate to demean myself, to submit to anyone, to humiliate myself, not to speak plainly, to give in, not to have my own way. Now as then, pride is present in whatever I do, in my gestures, in the hardness of my voice, in my steely gaze, in my anxious and well-developed facial features, in my entire being."

From her years at Aubazine (years in which she had no control over what happened to her and no control over her fate), there arose a fierce need to have her own way and to live the life she wanted to live, not the life that others wanted her to live.

ONE BRIGHT SPOT

During school holidays, Gabrielle and her sisters went to stay with their grandparents, Henri-Adrien and Virginie Chanel. The couple had given up the life of traveling merchants and had settled in Moulins, where they had their own stall in the town's covered market.

For Gabrielle, the best part of staying with her grandparents was the presence of their youngest daughter, Adrienne, who, though technically her aunt, was a girl of her own age. The two looked like sisters, had the natural sense of taste and refinement, shared an attic bedroom, and became quite inseparable, much to the dismay of Chanel's own sisters, who couldn't compete with Adrienne for their sister's attention.

Living not too far away from Chanel's grandparents was her aunt Louise, 19 years older than her own sister, Adrienne. And while Gabrielle may have learned the basics of sewing from the sisters at Aubazine, it was her aunt Louise who taught her how to do it with flair and imagination. Gabrielle learned how to sew straight pleats and to make fringes, how to dress up a simple blouse, and how to use remnants and bits of fabric as collars. In that simple

After the death of her mother and the disappearance of her father, Gabrielle was sent to live in the Aubazine orphanage *(above)*. Despite the bleak conditions, Gabrielle was provided with a proper education.

kitchen of the wife of a train stationmaster, Chanel made her first small steps toward being a designer.

In 1900, she turned 17. And since only girls who planned to become nuns were allowed to stay at Aubazine longer than that, Chanel returned to her aunt and uncle's home in Varennes, where she and Adrienne got jobs at a county fair, working at a candy stand while the owner took his wife to the hospital.

Two young, pretty girls selling candy were sure to get attention, and they quickly sold out their stock of bonbons and fudge, earning enough money to make a trip by train to Paris. That evening, they snuck out of the house and made their way to the station at Moulins, where no one knew them.

Adrienne, who took charge of the money, purchased two second-class tickets, but once aboard, Gabrielle decided she wanted more and insisted they both move up to the first-class seats. The pair were caught, and once they paid the first-class surcharge as well as a fine, they found themselves nearly penniless. Gabrielle would never recount what happened after that or how they managed to get back home.

THE *PENSIONNAT* AT MOULINS

Since both Gabrielle and Julie were too old to return to Aubazine, their grandmother sent them to the Notre Dame *pensionnat* at Moulins. The school, a finishing school for young ladies, took in a certain number of girls as "charity cases" who helped pay for their stay by working in the kitchen or performing other tasks. After one year, they were joined by their younger sister, Antoinette.

It was an age when young girls were not let out on their own, so Chanel's opportunities to explore life in Moulins were virtually nonexistent. Which, given the fact that she was a pretty girl and uneducated in the ways of the world, was perhaps not a bad thing. Moulins was a military garrison town, filled with young, single soldiers, most of whom were eager to find a good time with any available young girl.

The 10th Light Horse Regiment, which had served proudly in the Franco-Prussian War of 1870, was the most prominent. Dressed in scarlet pants and wearing peaked caps, the soldiers could be found at night throughout the town, looking for entertainment in one of the music halls where female singers performed patriotic songs or at the café-concerts, small cafés where orchestras performed in the evening and, on Sundays and holidays, where musical matinees took place.

By the age of 20, Chanel was ready to leave the confines of the Notre Dame boarding school and enter the world of Moulins. Besides the halls for entertaining the soldiers, Moulins was a town filled with tailor shops, where the young soldiers had their uniforms fitted and altered, and with pastry shops (*pâtisseries*), where visiting relatives and girlfriends could purchase sweet treats.

Gabrielle was allowed to join her aunt Adrienne as a shop assistant at a respectable establishment that specialized in lingerie

ELEMENTS OF STYLE

My hair is still black, rather like a horse's mane, my eyebrows are as black as our chimney sweep's, my skin is dark like the lava from our mountains, and my character is as black as the core of a land that has never capitulated. I was a rebellious child, a rebellious lover, a rebellious fashion designer, a true Lucifer.

—*from* Chanel and Her World: Friends, Fashion, and Fame
by Edmonde Charles-Roux

and hosiery, known as the House of Grampayre. Gabrielle and Adrienne lived with their employers above the shop, sharing a third-floor attic room.

At the House of Grampayre, the girls put their sewing skills to good use, while also helping to wait on the society ladies who came to purchase scarves and skirts, feather boas, mourning crepe, and sewing needs. Gabrielle resented the attitude of the shoppers who treated her as they would any other ordinary shopgirl.

In her later years, Chanel would conveniently forget the year and a half she spent at the House of Grampayre. Instead, she would tell interviewers of her life at her "aunt's," surrounded by pastures and grazing lands stocked with both dairy cows and horses. There, she said, gallant, handsome soldiers would come to ride, and she would worry that the soldiers would ride her favorites, horses she had ridden so hard earlier that their feet had been hurt.

None of this, of course, was true. But in her later years, Chanel was loathe to admit her humble beginnings as a shopgirl. Soldiers did in fact come into her life, but not by way of her nonexistent aunt's nonexistent horses, but at a tailor shop where she worked to earn extra money. It would become the beginning of a new life, of a way of escaping the life of "orphan" Gabrielle Chanel on the way to becoming Coco.

3

Becoming Coco

Now 21 years old, Gabrielle Chanel began to search for a life of her own, away from the protection of her employers. She took a small room on rue du pont Guinguet, and after some hesitation, Adrienne moved in with her, after getting her sister Louise's approval.

It quickly became known around Moulins that when women wanted to get their dresses altered, no one did it better than the two Chanel girls. The pair did work on their own and continued to work at the House of Grampayre, and on Sundays, Gabrielle also worked at the tailor shop to earn even more money. It was there, sometime during the 1904 racing season, that six dashing army lieutenants came into the shop on a Sunday afternoon for some last-minute alterations.

The lieutenants left with more than newly fitted attire. They invited both Gabrielle and Adrienne to join them later that afternoon

Gabrielle loved visiting her grandparents in the town of Moulins *(above)*, and after leaving the orphanage, she attended finishing school there. At Moulins, she fine-tuned her sewing skills.

to watch the jumping competition. The girls continued going out with the men; sometimes for sherbets, sometimes to pastry shops. Often Antoinette, now almost 16 years old, joined them as well.

They also went with the lieutenants to La Rotonde, the town's most elegant café; an eight-sided cast-iron pavilion where officers gathered nightly to listen to a female singer accompanied by an orchestra as well as to visiting comedy acts. And while it is not known whether one of the army officers dared her to or whether Gabrielle boasted of her singing abilities, it *is* known that the director of La Rotonde gave her the opportunity to get up on stage and sing; the audience was largely made up of her friends from the 10th Light Horse Regiment, who, despite the less-than-stellar quality of her voice, gave her a rousing ovation.

With her song, she earned more than the officers' applause. The song she sang, "Qui qu'a vu Coco?" about a Parisian woman who loses her dog at the Trocadero amusement park just across from the Eiffel Tower, gave her the nickname for which is known today.

ÉTIENNE BALSAN

Among the many officers she met during this period, one man stood out: Étienne Balsan. Balsan was the youngest of the three sons of a family whose fortune had been made in textiles. And while his two older brothers, Jacques and Robert, were the respectable members of the family who married well and worked hard to expand the family's business, Étienne had other things he wanted to do.

He had attended boarding school in England, where he developed a lifelong love of horses. So instead of following his brothers into the family business, his plan, after he left the military, was to purchase a property near Compiègne, at the edge of the Compiègne forest. There, he planned to ride and breed horses.

Balsan also had little interest in settling down to a respectable marriage like his older brothers. Instead, he found himself fascinated by the high-spirited Chanel, a young, beautiful girl living on her own. Although Balsan was not what one could call particularly good-looking, his down-to-earth nature impressed Chanel more than the more blue-blooded officers of the 10th Light Horse Regiment. The two became an item.

VICHY

By 1906, Moulins had, in Chanel's eyes, become too small to hold her big ambitions. She wanted more. She convinced Adrienne to go with her to the larger resort city of Vichy. There, she told her aunt, with their own newly designed wardrobes, they could work together and conquer the world of cafés and theaters.

Chanel aimed right for the top, auditioning at Vichy's most prestigious venue, the Grand Casino. On their way to the tryout, Adrienne and Gabrielle hired a photographer to take a picture of them standing in the park in their finery. It is the first known photograph of Gabrielle Chanel.

In it, one can see in her dress, one she had designed and made herself, the beginnings of the style that would become famous. The shoulders are square, with a large belt and relatively simple blouse (or shirtwaist as it was known), largely unadorned with just a hint of embroidery on the skirt and military braid on the shoulders. Compared to Adrienne's more traditional high-collared look, Grabielle's look is severe, almost masculine in style, set off and feminized with a frilly scarf.

But although Chanel had what Axel Madsen described as "presence and a certain acid charm," her voice was not nearly strong enough to get her hired as a singer. It was gently suggested to her that she could spice up her act by becoming a *gommeuse*, a woman who performed in a gaudy dress that showed off her cleavage and legs and allowed her to dance a few simple steps while singing. This was not quite what Chanel had in mind as a career.

She was saved by the arrival in Vichy of Étienne Balsan, who invited her to accompany him to the races to hear his big news. Balsan was now out of the army and had purchased the property he wanted, called Royallieu. He asked Chanel if she would like to go with him there to watch him train his racehorses.

It wasn't a particularly difficult decision. Her show business career was going nowhere. Adrienne had already given up and returned to Moulins, where she was living with Maud Mazuel, a respectable woman who served Adrienne as both chaperone and matchmaker. There was nothing holding her in Vichy.

There was one potential problem, though. Étienne Balsan already had a girlfriend who lived with him at Royallieu. But even that wasn't enough to stop Chanel from going with Balsan to his twelfth-century castle. She knew what her life would be like if she remained where she was, trying to earn a living in the small towns of provincial France. One thing she knew she *didn't* want was a life like her mother's, as a single mother traveling

The Father of Haute Couture

Curiously, it is an Englishman, Charles Frederick Worth (October 13, 1825–March 10, 1895), who is considered by many to be the father of haute couture, of high fashion.

Born in Bourne, Lincolnshire, England, Worth began his career working in several London drapery shops, before moving to Paris in 1846. He went to work for one of Paris's best-known drapery shops, Gagelin and Opigez, where he married one of the shop's models, Marie Vernet. Worth began to design dresses for his wife, and customers began to ask for copies of the dresses. He urged the owners of the company to expand into dressmaking, but when they resisted going into something considered as "low class" as dressmaking, Worth found an investor and went to work on his own.

The dressmaking establishment of Worth and Bobergh opened in 1858 and quickly made its mark, patronized by such notables as the French empress Eugénie, Austrian princess Pauline von Metternich, actress Sarah Bernhardt, and opera singer Nellie Melba. Patrons came from as far away as New York and Boston to be fitted and dressed in his creations.

He helped to redefine the female shape, emphasizing women's curves and draping them in rich fabrics. Worth achieved a series of notable firsts. He was the first designer to put labels into the clothes he manufactured. He was the first designer who displayed his clothing line four times a year at fashion shows. Rather than let the client order what *she* wanted, she chose a garment and fabric and had the dress fitted to her figure.

Worth was, in essence, the first true couturier, the man who revolutionized fashion, the first dressmaker to be considered an "artist" rather than a craftsman.

from one village market to another. Biographer Axel Madsen described her options:

> As an orphan without a dowry, she couldn't expect to attract honorable young men looking for a wife, but she was pretty enough to aspire to that other position that penniless young women aimed for—to find a protector.

ROYALLIEU

This period in European history was known as the Belle Époque (French for "beautiful age"). It began during the late nineteenth century and lasted until the beginning of World War I. Looking back, the Belle Époque is considered by many to be the golden age for the upper classes—Europe was at peace, new technologies were changing the lives of many, fortunes were there to be made. It was an era of elegant dress and style, when spa towns such as Deauville and Biarritz became easily accessible by railroad.

It was also a time before women's liberation, when opportunities for women were few and far between. A woman could, as Gabrielle Chanel had done in Moulins, work in a shop. If one was talented enough, she could perhaps work on the stage as an actress or a singer. But if a woman wanted more, and wanted to live a life of wealth and ease and was unable or unwilling to marry to do so, she might become a courtesan—a woman who, in exchange for luxuries, money, and status, gave her companionship to a rich and powerful man.

At Royallieu, Étienne Balsan had installed one of the era's most notorious and best-known courtesans—Émilienne d'Alençon. Amongher conquests had been the king of Belgium and Jacques d'Uzès, from whom she managed to snag his family's jewelry collection before his mother sent him away, out of Émilienne's clutches.

But by the time Chanel arrived at Royallieu, d'Alençon was 33 years old and past her peak. Indeed, to Étienne Balsan, she was, at this stage, more of a tourist attraction than a lover. So when Balsan brought Chanel home with him, d'Alençon, as well as the sportsmen, actresses, and horse aficionados who were his constant visitors, assumed that Chanel would be, in the words of Axel Madsen, a "new distraction for him."

Belle Époque fashion emphasized a formal look with high necks, long sleeves, cinched waists, and long, flowing skirts. Coco Chanel would change all that with her own modern style.

Gabrielle Chanel was not only a "new distraction" for Balsan; she was, in fact, a new kind of woman for him. She was what became known as a "Claudine," based on the popular fictional character created by the French writer Collette. A Claudine was a new woman, different from the overdressed, overstuffed women of the Belle Époque. She was a woman on the road to liberation, freer in her morals than the generation before her, a woman ready to toss away the fashionable corsets and stays that bound her figure tightly, ready to toss away the lace and silk and bustles and huge feathered and flowered hats that were all the rage, and replace them with clothes that were liberating, and to the Belle Époque eye, startling in their simplicity.

Chanel wasn't a writer or an artist, so she expressed herself the only way she knew how—through her clothes. As Axel Madsen described it,

> if ladies at the grandstand at Longchamp came in feather hats and skirts that swept the grass, she was at the racetrack in strict tailor-made and boater. If Dorziat [then an up-and-coming actress] came to the stables dressed in bias-cut to ride side-saddle, Gabrielle swung onto her horse wearing riding britches.

Life at Royallieu revolved around horses, horse racing, and racetracks. Mondays were spent at Saint-Cloud, Tuesdays at Enghien-les-Bains, Wednesdays at Tremblay, Thursdays at Auteuil, Fridays at Maisons-Laffitte, Saturdays at Vincennes, and, of course, Sundays were at Longchamp. To become one of the gang, Chanel took riding lessons, working in all weather conditions to get her riding up to snuff. She became fearless on horseback, and it was Balsan himself who taught her how to manage a horse in training.

Gabrielle was 22 years old when she came to live at Royallieu, and soon thereafter, Balsan's affair with Émilienne d'Aleçon was over. Her plush, if slightly aging, beauty couldn't compete with Chanel's slender youthfulness, her directness, and her sheer newness and novelty. During Chanel's time with Balsan, he would be involved with other women. Racehorses and women were his life, and whatever his feelings were for Gabrielle, he wasn't going to give up his interest in either.

He was intrigued with her, however, and remained so throughout her years with him and even afterward. She was unlike anyone he had ever met and dressed like no woman he had ever seen, in strikingly original clothes of her own design. She wore frocks she made herself, complete with a high collar and tie. She would wear a simple boater hat with her long hair held in place by a single hatpin—a look that combined the masculine with the feminine to achieve a kind of, as described by Axel Madsen, "reverse elegance."

She became, in an age when women were generally anything but, Balsan's friend. And since he was the first man to really take an interest in her and to show her the world outside of small villages and shops, she did what she could to please him and to keep him interested in her.

But there were limits. She had a role in his life, one that she was not allowed to overstep. She was, she knew, looked down on by the friends who came to visit, and Balsan himself refused to introduce her to "proper" society. For Chanel, it was a time of learning and a time of deep uncertainty. Always in the back of her mind was the knowledge that, just like Émilienne d'Alençon, she could easily be replaced by a younger and even newer girl.

Indeed, in her later years, Chanel would try to minimize the time she spent with Étienne and, eventually, to deny that those years actually took place. In the mythical life that she tried to present to the world, the life of an orphan who with the help of her "aunts" made her own way into the world, there was no place for the man who supported her financially for so many years.

By August 1908, at the age of 25, she found herself wondering more and more about what the future held for her. While Balsan tried to assure her that things were fine as they were, she wanted more. She knew that she couldn't earn a living riding

This portrait of Coco Chanel was taken around 1910.

ELEMENTS OF STYLE

Creation is an artistic gift, a collaboration of the couturier with his or her times. It is not by learning to make dresses that they become successful (making dresses and creating fashion are different things); fashion does not exist only in dresses; fashion is in the air, it is borne on the wind, you can sense it, you can breathe it, it's in the skin and on the highway, it's everywhere, it has to do with ideas, with social mores, with events.

—from Chanel and Her World: Friends, Fashion, and Fame
by Edmonde Charles-Roux

horses. At the same time, she knew that she wanted to work. But what could she do?

One thing she knew she could do, and that others would respond to, was design hats. It may seem impossible to imagine today, when women's hats have gone the way of the horse and carriage, but in those days, a woman simply did not leave the house without a proper hat. Large hats, embellished with fanciful feathers, artificial birds and flowers, and whatever else one could possibly imagine, were seen everywhere.

Chanel's hats were different. Her look was a simple bowler, a round, hard, felt hat with a narrow brim. When Coco wore one of her hats to the racetrack, decorated simply with ribbons and lace, she caused a sensation. Several of Balsan's female friends had asked her to create hats for them as well. Even Émilienne had been seen wearing one of Chanel's hats at Longchamp. Perhaps, Gabrielle suggested to Balsan, he could provide the financial backing so that she could open up her own millinery store in Paris.

This was a first for Étienne Balsan. Other women had asked him for clothing, for jewels, for money, even for cars. Nobody had ever asked him for his help in opening a business. He was not necessarily opposed to the idea, and he had an empty apartment in Paris that she was free to use, but he still had several questions. How would they arrange it? Would the business be in her name or in his? Did she want him to just give her the money, as he had so often done with women of her kind, or would it be a loan?

Instead of giving her an answer right away, he stalled. He had been invited to attend a fox hunt at a thirteenth-century château in Pau, in the heart of the Pyrenees. Chanel, who had never been to that part of France, agreed to accompany him. She had no idea that the decision would not only clear the way for her to open her own business, but it also would lead her to the man who would become the love of her life.

4

Rue Cambon

Gabrielle Chanel met Arthur "Boy" Capel at Pau, where she had accompanied Balsan on his foxhunting expedition. Chanel was immediately drawn to Capel by the way he smelled. All her life, she had been known for having a particularly sensitive sense of smell, and Capel's ever-present aroma of horses, leather, the outdoors, and saddle soap was one that she found very attractive.

There was more to her attraction, of course, than just the way he smelled. Chanel was drawn to his good looks, his confidence, and his easygoing nature. There was also a striking difference between Capel and Balsan. While Balsan always seemed to like horses more than he did people, Capel was interested in people. So interested, in fact, that people were immediately drawn to him by his obvious interest in their lives.

By 1910, Chanel was ready to open her own business, with backing from Étienne Balsan.

Chanel left Balsan for Capel, writing him a note that, according to Paul Madsen, simply said, "I am leaving with Boy Capel. Forgive me, but I love him." She went to the train station without knowing for sure whether Capel wanted her to join him or not. Capel was drawn to Chanel by her singular looks, her honesty, her charm, her somewhat unconventional taste, and her dislike for anything phony. The fact that she was also Balsan's mistress only made her all the more alluring and desirable.

When Chanel and Capel arrived in Paris, they went to his apartment on L'avenue Gabriel and began their relationship. Capel, the son of a wealthy Catholic British family, spoke fluent French and was one year older than Chanel. But although he was wealthy, he was not nearly as wealthy as Étienne Balsan.

Fortunately for all parties concerned, Étienne Balsan was definitely not the jealous type. In fact, upon his return from Argentina, he agreed to help Chanel open her millinery shop and invited Chanel and Boy Capel back to Royallieu for a visit. It was the first time she had seen him since leaving to be with Capel, but Balsan seemed to take the new relationship in stride. Not only did he welcome the couple into his home, but he also kept his word on his offer: Chanel would still be able to use his apartment in Paris for her shop, and he would still finance her business.

Chanel and Capel were often invited to parties at Royallieu. At one of them, they engaged in an elaborate masquerade: The actress Jeanne Levy was dressed up as a bride; Étienne Balsan, in top hat and tails, as the groom. Boy Capel was the mother of the bride, dressed in a simple dress and one of Chanel's own hats. Chanel herself was the best man, wearing a costume she put together from boy's clothing. As her biographer, Axel Madsen, put it, "The beginning of her life's work was in this tomboy creation, in the feminizing of masculine fashions."

FIRST SUCCESS

Chanel worked out of Balsan's apartment on Le boulevard Malesherbes and lived with Capel in L'avenue Gabriel. Her hat shop was an immediate success. She purchased inexpensive, flat-topped straw hats and boaters from Galeries Lafayette, a department store, and decorated and trimmed them herself, turning plain hats into a Chanel fashion statement.

Her first customers, perhaps surprisingly, were largely the former girlfriends of Étienne Balsan. Those women, pleased by her designs, would in turn bring in *their* friends. Other women took notice of the new look in hats and began flocking to the shop, wanting one for themselves. To wear a Chanel hat, so simple and

The Man Who Listened to Chanel

Paul Morand (March 13, 1888–July 24, 1976) was more than the man whom Chanel trusted enough to tell her life story (true and not-so-true versions).

A graduate of the Paris Institute of Political Studies, he was a diplomat, novelist, playwright, poet, and friend of many of France's greatest writers and artists, including novelist Marcel Proust.

Known for his stylish writing and his novel, *Lewis et Irène*, largely based on the relationship between Chanel and Boy Capel, his reputation was severely damaged during World War II. An outspoken anti-Semite, he collaborated with the Vichy regime (the French government that existed during the Nazi occupation and which collaborated with the Germans to a high degree). When the war ended, Morand, who was serving the Vichy government as ambassador to Switzerland, was released from his position, and it was there in exile that Morand started his collaboration with Chanel on her never-to-be memoirs.

elegant compared to the typical woman's hat of the time, was definitely an act of defiance; a way of making a statement. And Chanel worked tirelessly to make her business a success.

At the same time, Boy Capel was working hard to make his own family business—coal mining—an even greater success. It was a new world for Chanel, to live with a man who was determined to make his fortune rather then spend it. When they weren't working, the couple was often seen at the city's best restaurants: Maxim's, the Café de Paris, and Pré Catelan. Capel introduced Chanel to a world she had never known, one of English lords and Russian dukes—the world of high society. She was both fascinated and appalled by what she saw.

Chanel never lost her fascination with Boy Capel. To the end of her life, he was the one man about whom she mainly told the truth, the one she talked about, the one she truly loved. "We were made for each other," Axel Madsen quotes her as insisting toward the end of her life. "That he was there and that he loved me, and that he knew I loved him was all that mattered."

A HISTORIC MOVE

It was Boy Capel who advanced Chanel the money that allowed her to move her business from Étienne Balsan's apartment to the address she would be linked to for the rest of her life: rue Cambon. It was an ideal location for her: a neighborhood of chic women's shops, of the world-famous L'hôtel Ritz Paris, and of government buildings.

She rented space at number 21 and decorated it with things taken from Capel's apartment. It was her chance to build a successful business, to prove to herself that she could be a success, and that she could do it on her own. As quoted by Madsen, Chanel told Capel, "I'll know that I love you when I don't need you anymore."

But for the time being, she *did* need him. While she had an innate sense of fashion, of what worked and what didn't work to make a woman look her best, she didn't yet know how to run a business. On one occasion, when Capel told her that she had been allowed to write overdrafts on her business account only because he had made the deposits to back them up, she threw her purse in his face and ran out of the restaurant into a rainstorm, embarrassed and humiliated by her lack of knowledge and her dependence on Capel.

The very next day, she set out to learn everything she needed to run the business on her own, telling her assistant that fun time was over. "I'm here to make a fortune," she told her, according to Madsen. "Henceforth, nobody spends a centime [a French cent] without my permission."

She began to become known and to be noticed, not necessarily just for her designs, but for her personality, somewhat to Chanel's

Chanel and Arthur "Boy" Capel lounge on the beach in Saint Jean de Luz in 1917. Chanel depended on Capel to help her run her young business.

discomfort. Chanel was, at this early stage of her career, a mixture of naïveté and ambition. She still viewed herself as a simple country girl from the provinces, yet she aspired to dress some of France's most fashionable and wealthy women. For decades, those women had gone to the designers Frederick Worth, Jacques Doucet, and Paul Poiret—designers who had dressed Europe's and America's most fashionable women in the most stylish clothes of their age, clothes that emphasized the female figure and that were elaborate, richly designed, and, frankly, uncomfortable to wear and move in. By 1913, having established herself as a hat designer to be reckoned with, Chanel was ready to take on the world of high fashion.

CHANEL INVENTS WOMEN'S SPORTSWEAR

She had begun to slowly introduce clothing into her shop on rue Cambon—knitted polo shirts similar to the ones that Boy Capel wore when he played polo, along with simple sweaters and blazers. The time for these fashions, with their practical, almost masculine look, hadn't yet come—it was still the time for frills, lace, and exaggerated femininity.

But by 1913, Chanel's time had come. The shop on rue Cambon was doing well—so well, in fact, that it was no longer necessary for Capel to back up the shop's credit himself. Chanel was now able to succeed on her own and at last had the feeling that she had become an adult able to take care of herself.

Well, perhaps not entirely capable of taking care of herself. In the summer of 1913, with Capel's financial backing, Gabrielle Chanel decided to open up her first boutique. It would be located on the Normandy coast at the seaside resort of Deauville, on La rue Gontaut-Biron, one of the town's chicest addresses. There, in the playground of France's well-to-do, Chanel would make her first big splash in fashion.

Naturally, the shop carried the simple hats that Chanel had introduced in Paris, but she wanted to do more. Women's clothing was beginning to change with the times—designers were getting rid of the confining corset and high collars of the Belle Époque but were making up for it with an excess of feathers and bright colors. Her idea was to simplify and pare things down even further.

As Chanel biographer Axel Madsen pointed out, her millinery had been a reaction against the "walking fruit bowls" of the day that passed for hats. Now, she wanted to do the same for women's attire—to take it from the excess that had been the fashion and bring it down to its function as elegant, practical, and easy-to-wear clothing. With the assistance of two 16-year-old girls, she went to work.

She made clothing designed to be worn while on vacation, clothing designed for relaxation and living outdoors. It was sports fashion for women; clothing designed for Chanel's own needs and sense of style and introduced to an audience that, as it turned out, was ready to make a change.

It was informal clothing, meant to be worn without a corset or stays. She took her look where she found it—turtleneck sweaters worn by English sailors in port, for example, or the polo shirts

The Chanel flagship store sits at 29 rue Cambon in Paris, not far from Chanel's early store on the avenue.

I was extremely naïve. I didn't begin to imagine that I was of interest to people; I didn't realize that it was me they were looking at. I thought of myself merely as a country girl, like so many others. The age of extravagant dresses, those dresses worn by heroines that I had dreamt about, was past . . . I no longer thought about lace; I knew that extravagant things didn't suit me. All I kept were my goat-skin coat and my simple outfits.

"Since you are so attached to them," Capel said to me, "I'm going to get you to have the clothes you have always worn remade elegantly, by an English tailor."

Everything to do with rue Cambon stemmed from there.

—*from* Chanel and Her World: Friends, Fashion, and Fame
by Edmonde Charles-Roux

worn by Capel. Instead of the expensive and stiff fabrics that meant "high fashion," she used simpler fabrics, such as knits and flannels. These were fabrics more often associated with men's clothing and English schoolboy uniforms, but it confirmed her view, quoted by Axel Madsen, that a look "has everything to do with elegance but is based on elements alien to elegance—comfort, ease, and common sense."

Other clothes were soon added—jumpers, jackets, and the sailor blouse known as the *marinière* that within a year would become *the* garment for well-dressed ladies. She would send her aunt Adrienne out every day, strolling along the beach in Chanel's newest creations, causing a stir and bringing growing numbers of buyers into Chanel's boutique. There, they saw clothes they had never seen before—simple gray and navy jersey dresses, jackets, and even, for the first time in women's fashion, bathing suits made from the same material as Boy Capel's sweaters. It was the beginning of a clothing revolution for women. And Gabrielle Chanel was there on the front lines.

Now 30 years old, she was becoming a celebrity. She was photographed standing on the beach wearing an oversize sweater with pushed-up sleeves, pockets, and a belt, over a blouse and ankle-length skirt. "Everybody wanted to meet me," she would say years later, as quoted by Madsen. "I became something of a celebrity, and there, too, I started a fashion—couturiers as stars. Before my time, that didn't exist."

That summer of 1914 was a golden time for Gabrielle Chanel. Her first clothing line was a big success, and her relationship with Capel, despite his frequent absences and the rumors of him being with other women, was flourishing. But the world was sliding toward war, and with the outbreak of World War I that August, the old Belle Époque ended and a new, very different world was about to begin. A world that, as it turned out, was ready for the changes that Chanel was introducing.

5

The Great War
and First Success

There were record crowds in Deauville that summer of 1914 when on June 28 Archduke Franz Ferdinand, the heir to the Austrian throne, was assassinated in Sarajevo, triggering World War I. Country after country began mobilizing for war, and by August 1, Russia and Germany were officially at war. That same day, the French government announced that it, too, would begin to mobilize its troops. Two days later, Germany declared war on France, and the resort community of Deauville emptied. Chanel, who thought of little but her boutique, was convinced that the Kaiser had declared war on France just to make her life difficult.

Capel convinced Chanel to keep the shop open. Britain declared war on Germany, and German troops moved through Belgium and crossed into France, quickly approaching the capi-

Chanel's mix of feminine and masculine created an alluring new style for women.

tal city of Paris. Boy Capel was called into service. The Germans occupied Royallieu, and for a time it seemed that France would quickly fall to the German onslaught. But French and British troops fought back at the Battle of the Marne, the German offense was stopped, and a long period of brutal trench warfare began.

For Gabrielle Chanel in Deauville, however, things couldn't have been better. The city, which had become a virtual ghost town with the first hints of war, had quickly filled up with panic-stricken, wealthy Parisian women fleeing from the German attack with little but the clothes on their back. They would all need to buy new clothing, especially attire they could wear while keeping busy doing volunteer work at hospitals and such to help the war effort.

Coco Chanel's boutique was the only fine women's clothing shop open in Deauville. And her clothing, described by Axel Madsen as "sporty clothes . . . just right for physical activities— oversized, hip-length knit jackets and straight linen skirts, sailor's blouses with open collars and hats devoid of decoration," were just what the times required. Chanel's shop was swamped with buyers; it was so busy that Gabrielle was forced to summon her aunt Adrienne back from Paris to help out.

But by the end of the year, Gabrielle, wanting to be closer to Boy, returned to Paris along with Adrienne and the rest of the French aristocracy, leaving a saleswoman in charge of the Deauville boutique. The city she returned to was one that, with the exception of young boys and old men, was largely dominated by women. These were women freed from the restraints of prewar Paris, upper-class women who were now forced to live without servants, and other women forced to go work in munitions factories and hospitals. Women who needed, not the overdone fashion of the prewar era, but clothing that moved and that they could work in.

They needed sports clothing and jerseys. Because of fabric shortages, hemlines were higher, and because of metal shortages, stays finally disappeared forever. So while Boy Capel shuttled back and forth on mysterious missions between Paris and London, Chanel worked to design clothing to meet the more somber, practical, wartime mood. Gone were the curves of the prewar period. In its place, Chanel offered slimness. Madsen quotes her as saying:

The Chanel Sweater

One of Chanel's most popular looks became known as the Chanel sweater. Where did it come from?

In the most likely version of the story of its creation, Chanel was cold and picked up a man's polo player sweater to wear. Because the sweater was too large for her, to adjust the fit, she pushed up the sleeves and tightened it around her body with a belt. The look, she thought, was becoming and one that could work for other women as well.

She was right. After its introduction at the Deauville boutique, it became an immediate sensation, a look worn by many women throughout the World War I era, written about in *Vogue*, and imitated by designers everywhere.

I let go of the waistline and came up with a new silhouette. To get into it, and with the war's connivance, all my clients lost weight, "to become skinny like Coco." Wearing Coco Chanel clothes makes you look young, they said.

It was a new, slim look—a new way of looking feminine. It was accompanied by another shocking departure in which Chanel led the way. For decades, a woman was defined by her long, flowing hair. The style was impossible to maintain while working in a factory or hospital. Chanel began to gradually cut her hair shorter and shorter, until it reached the stage where it was said she looked like a young boy. And other women soon followed her example.

ANOTHER SUCCESSFUL SHOP

With the war dragging on, many in Parisian high society began looking for a new place to escape from an increasingly dreary and war-tired Paris. Many moved their base of operations to Spain, which remained neutral and did not take sides in the war. There, on the beautiful Riviera, Biarritz became the place to be. Naturally, Gabrielle Chanel followed the crowds.

Boy Capel provided the funds to rent a villa across from the famous casino. Chanel's sister Antoinette was brought in, along with some of rue Cambon's best seamstresses. On July 15, 1915, Chanel opened the first fashion house Biarritz had ever seen.

The house was an immediate success, and before long, Chanel had 60 girls working for her. One of them was Marie-Louise Deray, who years later would recall how difficult it was to keep up with Chanel's demands, as quoted by Madsen.

> We worked with jersey, a fabric that no one had dared use before to make dresses. The "diagonals" went every which way and we had to start over again several times. Mademoiselle was demanding. If a fitting went wrong she exploded. She loved to pester people. I cried a lot, believe me. She was tough, unrelenting from the staff. But what she came up with was sensational, both chic and exceedingly simple, so different from Poiret and Madeline Vionnet.

Her way of working was different than Poiret's or Vionnet's as well. Unlike most designers, Chanel had no interest or talent for sketching her designs first. Instead, after she had selected the materials she wanted to work with, she would explain in great detail to her staff exactly what she wanted. Then, after they came up with a rough version, she went to work herself.

The rough version would be put on the mannequin or a live model, who would have to stand for an excruciatingly long and boring six to seven hours while Chanel fitted the clothes, cutting, altering, adding, and changing as she went along. Sometimes it would take up to 30 fittings before Chanel achieved the look she wanted. Her models were poorly paid, receiving only 100 francs a month, although one dress sold for as much as 7,000 francs. Despite this she refused to raise their salaries, saying, according to Amy De La Haye and Shelley Tobin, "They're beautiful girls. Let them take lovers."

Chanel is photographed here circa 1920 wearing her signature multi-strand pearls.

And while she may not have had the technical expertise of some other designers, she had something they didn't, something that couldn't be learned or taught—an instinctive feel for fashion and for what worked on a woman's body. She chose all the materials herself—the lace, the accessories, the colors. And, because she worked directly on a model, her clothes did something that other's did not: They *moved*—freely, easily, and naturally. It was clothing designed for a modern woman, one freed from the restraints of the previous century.

And women and critics noticed. By 1915, the leading magazine, *Harper's Bazaar*, proclaimed, according to De La Haye and Tobin, that "the woman who hasn't at least one Chanel is hopelessly out of the running in fashion." One year later, that same magazine was the first in America to publish a picture of a Chanel design: A dress without a collar or bodice, but worn with a deep V-cut in front underneath a men's style vest or waistcoat. Topping the look was a large hat decorated with a simple twist of fur. The caption, quoted by Madsen, simply described it as "Chanel's charming chemise dress."

By 1917, *Vogue* was reporting that her jersey dresses were being worn in Palm Beach. New, looser-fitting styles with sashes and belts draped around the hips were being seen that spring, leading *Harper's* to state, as quoted by De La Haye and Tobin, that "this season the name of Gabrielle Chanel is on the lips of every buyer." Antoinette was safely in charge of the boutique in Biarritz, and Chanel herself moved among her three shops, supervising a total staff of 300.

THE ARTISTIC WORLD OF PARIS

In May 1917, Gabrielle Chanel met Marie Sophie Olga Zénaïde Godebska—the actress known as Misia Sert. This remarkable woman became one of Coco's best friends. She was a pianist who played for ballet director Sergei Diaghilev, and who knew and modeled for such painters as Henri de Toulouse-Lautrec, Pierre-Auguste Renoir, Édouard Vuillard, and Pierre Bonnard. It was through Misia that Chanel gained a love of things Russian and was introduced to the artistic world of Paris.

They met at a dinner held by Paul Morand. Misia was immediately drawn to Chanel and was quoted by Madsen as remembering years later that "despite the fact that she did not say a word, she radiated a charm I found irresistible." Misia was in the midst of fundraising for Diaghilev's famous dance company, the Ballet Russe, at that time, trapped outside of its native Russia by war and revolution.

On May 17, with the assistance of Misia, Diaghilev premiered his new work *Parade*, with music by composer Erik Satie and sets by the man who became known as perhaps the twentieth century's most influential artist, Pablo Picasso. It was the artistic event of the season, and there in attendance were Boy Capel and Coco Chanel, stylish in her short, bobbed hair and clothing of her own design.

Although Chanel had mixed feelings about the ballet itself— "It was too new, and it scared me. I asked myself, Is this beautiful?"—she attended the dinner afterward, where, as described by Axel Madsen, she met Picasso for the first time. "He was nasty then, but he fascinated me. He watched you like a hawk ready to swoop down on its prey. He scared me. When he came into a room and I didn't see him, yet I knew he was watching me."

For the first time, a fashion designer, previously seen by society as just a "tradesperson," little different from a butcher or shopkeeper, had left the anonymity of the workshop to become a celebrity in her own right. The independent and unique Chanel and the dashing Capel were seen in all the best places.

Capel was now the author of the best-selling book *Reflections on Liberty: A Project for the Federation of Governments*, which was a proposal for rebuilding Europe when the war ended. Chanel was also getting rich. With the price of coal setting record highs, demand for fur in fashion skyrocketed, and Coco was only too happy to oblige. Her jersey costumes trimmed with fur made her a fortune, but, given wartime shortages, as Madsen quotes British *Vogue*, it was best that women "not inquire too closely into the origins of some of the strange skins which have been cut into strips or folded into collars to trim many of the smartest frocks."

Much to Boy Capel's unhappiness, Chanel was becoming independent of him. She had earned enough money to pay him back all the money she owed him, as well as to purchase the villa in Biarritz from him for 300,000 francs—all in cash. She was also moving away from him socially, becoming friends with Pablo Picasso and his wife, Russian composer Igor Stravinsky, writer Jean Cocteau, and poet Raymond Radiguet. It was a world that Capel was not entirely comfortable with, and for the first time, he found himself becoming jealous of Coco and her business and social success.

THE END OF A RELATIONSHIP

There was soon another woman. Traveling to the front line at Arras, Capel had met ambulance driver Diana Lister Wyndham, the daughter of Lord Ribblesdale. A recent widow, the beautiful 25-year-old could give Capel things, as Axel Madsen stated, that Coco could not: "a brilliant marriage, conventionality, aristocratic connections." The two fell in love, and soon Capel had to give the news to Chanel: He and Wyndham were engaged to be married.

It was the end of an eight-year-long relationship. Little is known of Chanel's reaction to the news of Capel's relationship. The couple remained together for several months, even after the official announcement, before Chanel moved into an apartment of her own, one with views of the river Seine from her window.

On September 29, 1918, Germany, whose troops had been pushed back with the entry of U.S. troops, asked the Allies for an armistice. The next month, Captain Arthur Capel married Diana Lister Wyndham. One month later, on November 11, an armistice was signed, ending one of the bloodiest wars in history. Eight-and-a-half million men had died, including more than one million Frenchmen and almost one million soldiers of the British Empire. Hundreds of thousands remained disabled, and much of Europe was in ruins. With the end of what became known as The Great War, and the end of her relationship with Capel, it was time for Chanel, as well as Europe, to reassess and rebuild.

Sportswear, such as the ensemble worn by Chanel here, became all the rage, as it allowed women to participate in more active lifestyles than they previously had.

ELEMENTS OF STYLE

In 1914, there were no sports dresses. Women attended sporting occasions rather as fifteenth-century ladies in conical hats attended tournaments. They wore very low girdles, and they were bound at the hips, legs, everywhere . . . Since they ate a great deal, they were stout, and since they were stout and didn't want to be, they strapped themselves in. The corset pushed the fat up to the bosom and hid it beneath the dress. By inventing the jersey, I liberated the body, I discarded the waist (and only reverted to it in 1930), I created a new shape; in order to conform to it all my customers, with the help of the war, became slim, "slim like Coco." Women came to me to buy their slim figures. "With Coco, you're young, do as she does," they would say to their suppliers. To the great indignation of couturiers, I shortened dresses. The jersey in those days was only worn underneath; I gave it the honour of being worn on top.

—*from* Chanel and Her World: Friends, Fashion, and Fame
by Edmonde Charles-Roux

AFTER THE WAR

Despite the tragic losses, life slowly returned to normal. Although northern France was in ruins, and the nation was nearly broke with debts that would be nearly impossible to pay, slowly but surely Paris began to revive. Artists, students, painters, and writers all began to flock to Paris—drawn by its beauty, its openness to new ideas, and its culture.

And Gabrielle Chanel was there, ready to dress the women of Paris, of France, of Europe, and of the world in clothing that could be described as functional chic. The line of her clothing, which closely followed the body's natural lines, made the clothing of every other designer look old-fashioned and overdone. As *Vogue* said, as quoted by Madsen, "Everything she does makes news—

the first quilted coat, the narrow crepe de chine dress inside a cage of tulle, and the suntan which she cultivates."

While other designers such as Edward Molyneux were showing women's eveningwear of long dresses and hats with ostrich feathers, Chanel was finding her market in the area between sportswear and formal afternoon clothing. With the end of the war, summer weekends were becoming fashionable again. These weekends included driving, swimming, sailing, tennis, and other such activities.

The fashion magazines sent out the message loud and clear: The well-dressed woman's weekend wardrobe was not complete without a "traveling suit" made from wool jersey paired with a neatly tailored blouse, day dresses, sports dresses, and pair after pair of low-heeled shoes, all available at Coco Chanel's boutiques. Chanel's "poor look" may have been expensive, but it was designed to make whoever wore it look both young and casual, the look that, as the 1920s began, was the *look* that every stylish woman aimed for.

At the same time, even though Arthur Capel had married Diana Wyndham—who was now pregnant with his child—he was still not willing to give up his relationship with Coco Chanel entirely. He would often come to visit her, to stay with her, to tell her how unhappy he was, and that he wanted his old life with her back. After one such visit, he announced that he was driving south to Cannes, to spend the Christmas holidays with his wife and sister. It was the last time Chanel would ever see Capel.

On the night of December 22, the news was brought to Chanel that Arthur Capel had been in a car accident. A tire had burst, the car had overturned, and Boy had been killed in the resulting blaze. Chanel refused to cry. She simply went to her bedroom to pack an overnight bag, and early that morning, she set off on the long drive to Cannes.

She arrived in Cannes late Christmas Day but was too late to attend the funeral, which, because of the holiday, had taken place the day before. Wanting to pay her respects, she was driven to the spot to see where the fatal accident had taken place. The burned-out shell of Capel's car was still there.

The chauffeur later told Capel's sister, Lady Bertha Michelham, what happened. Chanel got out of the car, walked over to the wreckage, and reached out to touch it, running her hands over it like a blind person. She then sat down on a nearby road marker and cried.

6

Tragedy and Triumph

Arthur Capel had been the great love of Gabrielle Chanel's life, and now he was gone. Chanel told Paul Morand that, although at the time of Capel's death he had been married to another woman, in her mind Chanel felt that *she* was his widow. She turned her bedroom into a room of mourning: black sheets, black curtains, and black drapes. But she soon tired of playing the "widow" and bought a new house in the wealthy Parisian suburb of Garches. There, with her faithful staff of Joseph and Marie and their daughter, in addition to two terriers that had been Boy's last gifts to her, she retired to mourn her lost love.

Her great friend Misia would have none of it. Paris was filling up with wealthy Russian émigrés who had fled the Russian Revolution, the arts were having a grand resurgence in the war's aftermath, and Misia, who knew and was friends with both the aristocrats *and* the artists, wanted to get Chanel out of the suburbs and back into the midst of life in Paris.

But even Misia couldn't open every door in Paris. When Étienne and Edith de Beaumont, two members of the aristocracy who also lived in the world of the avant-garde artists, threw a costume ball and did not invite Chanel, Misia refused to attend as well. Later, as quoted by Madesn, she recalled, "I know perfectly well that in those days society would never dream of inviting its 'tradespeople,' and the latter never allow themselves to recognize you or greet you outside your house."

It would take years before Chanel had become so big a star, so powerful a personality, that the Beaumonts were begging her to attend their parties. Chanel would attend those parties because

Misia Sert poses for Henri de Toulouse-Lautrec in this photograph. Sert introduced Chanel to many artists and artistrocats in Paris.

they served to introduce her to ever higher levels of society, but, as quoted by Axel Madsen, she never forgot or forgave their previous attitude. "All those bluebloods, they turned their noses up at me, but I'll have them groveling at my feet," she promised.

CHANEL AND THE ARTS

Through Misia, she began to expand her connections in the world of the arts. She met the great Russian composer Igor Stravinsky in May 1921. When Misia married the Spanish artist José-María Sert y Badia, Chanel accompanied them on their honeymoon in Italy, where she met the Russian ballet impresario Sergey Diaghilev, who, still feeling the effects of the war and revolution, was attempting to raise funds for a revival of his most famous production, *Le sacre du printemps* (*The Rite of Spring*).

Weeks later, Diaghilev was in Paris, where he was told that a Mademoiselle Chanel was looking for him. Meeting him in the lobby of his hotel, Chanel informed him that she had been thinking about his difficulties and wanted to help. Her biographers differ on the amount, but she then gave him a check of somewhere between 200,000 and 300,000 francs—a large sum of money no matter how one looks at it.

With that, she became a supporter of the arts, a role that gave her even greater access to both the world of the artist and of the aristocracy. When the new production of *The Rite of Spring* opened on December 15, 1921, Chanel was invited to the afterparty, which was attended by such luminaries as Diaghilev, Picasso, the Serts, and the composer Stravinsky, whose music had accompanied the ballet. Stravinsky was there in another role as well. Despite being married, he had also begun a relationship with Coco Chanel.

Chanel was also the designer whose name was on everybody's lips. For 1921, her look was sweaters, short, pleated skirts with dropped waistlines, and cloche ("bell") hats. The age of the flapper was starting. Flappers were "liberated" woman of the 1920s who wore short skirts and had short "bobbed" hair, listened to jazz music, and broke the rules of what was considered "proper" for young women. They wore too much makeup, drank, drove fast cars, and ignored the social and sexual norms of the time. In France, the look was called the Garçonne Look, taken from Victor Margueritte's sensational novel *La Garçonne* (The Bachelor Girl), about a young woman who leaves her family home to build an independent life for herself.

And while Chanel may not have, as she later insisted, "invented" the flapper (or the Garçonne), she certainly told her what to wear. Chanel was, in fact, the first person to truly design clothing for the young. As her biographer Axel Madsen points out, "The quintessential 1920s woman—slim, sophisticated, streamlined, and

Pablo Picasso and Igor Stravinsky

If it was Gabrielle Chanel who helped to liberate women's fashion from the constraints of the nineteenth century and bring it strongly into the twentieth century, it was two of her friends, Pablo Picasso and Igor Stravinsky, who did the same with painting and music.

Pablo Ruiz y Picasso (October 25, 1881–April 8, 1973) was the twentieth century's best-known artist. Painting in a variety of styles, starting with realism and on through a series of different techniques, theories, and ideas, he liberated art from the realism that had prevailed for centuries. This allowed artists to put on canvas what they saw or felt, not just a literal representation of a physical object.

In his most famous artistic period, known as Cubism, a representation of a physical object is broken up, reassembled, and shown, not just from one perspective or point of view, but from multiple viewpoints at the same time. It is a more complex view of art and reality, and one that Picasso helped to introduce to the world.

modern—didn't so much demand a fashion that was 'boyish' as one that was youthful." For perhaps the first time in history, women didn't strive to look "grown-up." As young people began to lead more independent lives, they became the ones who set the trends. And the trend was definitely going Chanel's way.

Critics raved about her look, Madsen quotes: "Chanel is making us forget yesterday's woman, teaching us to walk naturally, by snipping a lock here, the flounces of a dress there." What she did in fashion is by today's standards perfectly sensible, but by 1920s standards, it caused an earthquake. Simply put, she threw away the complicated, uncomfortable clothes of previous eras and replaced them with a stripped-down, uncluttered, casual look—one that is

At the same time that Picasso was revolutionizing art, Igor Fyodorovich Stravinsky (June 17, 1892–April 6, 1971), composer, pianist, and conductor, was doing the same thing for music. Russian born, Stravinsky is still best known for the three ballet scores commissioned by impresario Sergey Diaghilev for his Ballets Russes: *Firebird* (1910), *Petrushka* (1911), and *Le sacre du printemps* (*The Rite of Spring*) (1913).

It is this last piece in particular that caused the biggest uproar. It premiered on May 13, 1913, an occasion attended by the elite of Paris, including Gabrielle Chanel. The opening notes of Stravinsky's score, a bassoon solo backed by ominously discordant chords that soon developed into a never-before-heard assault of dissonant rhythms and violent and percussive sounds, accompanying ballet star Vaslav Nijinsky's startling choreography caused a reaction that Stravinsky could never have predicted.

Beginning with catcalls and whistles, it soon developed into a free-for-all of face slapping, fistfighting, and chair throwing. The shock of the new can sometimes cause that reaction. But today, *The Rite of Spring* is viewed as an essential piece of music, and Stravinsky as the man who helped bring classical music, kicking and screaming, into the twentieth century.

still seen everywhere today and is still synonymous with her name. The fashions she designed throughout the 1920s are what made her name and are clothes that, with some minor changes, remain stylish.

HER RUSSIAN PERIOD

Her relationship with Stravinsky did not last, but in what she called her "Slavic period," she moved on to her next relationship, with Grand Duke Dmitri Pavlovich, the grandson of Czar Alexander II, nephew of Czar Alexander III, and cousin of the last czar, Nicholas II. It was an unlikely relationship for the abandoned daughter of an itinerant peddler who was at that time, more than likely, as described by Edmonde Charles-Roux, still selling suspenders and handkerchiefs from his pushcart at "2 francs a dozen."

And while this relationship did not last either, this "Slavic period" did have an effect on her clothes. She took the traditional Russian blouse, a long, belted *rubachka*, and made it, in the words of Charles-Roux, "the uniform of chic Parisiennes." She took tunics and skirts and embroidered them with chain stitching that gave them a distinctive "Russian" look. These embroidered dresses proved to be so popular that she built a workshop entirely dedicated to embroidery.

She began designing costumes for the theater, the first for a landmark production of the Greek drama *Antigone*, adapted by Jean Cocteau, featuring the avant-garde writer Antonin Artaud, a score by Arthur Honegger, and stage designs by Pablo Picasso. The production received rave notices and ran for 100 performances. It was one more step in a remarkable career as Gabrielle Chanel transformed herself into "Chanel," with all the glamour and allure that that name conjures. As Axel Madsen put it, "Coco was inventing her personage."

But despite her fame as a person and as a personality, it was her fashions that truly fascinated the public. Alone among designers of the day, she knew the importance of the way clothes fit and the way they moved on a woman's body. She knew that the goal of women's fashion was to make a woman look beautiful, and that's what her clothes, with their classic simplicity, did.

Chanel was the best publicity for her own fashions. She was stylish by nature, and women wanted to copy her style.

CHANEL AT FORTY

Chanel's Christmas party of 1922 only served to solidify her position in Parisian society. One prominent guest, quoted by Axel Madsen, said, "Unlike certain salons where the champagne is not exactly vintage, the caviar and champagne amassed at Mademoiselle Chanel's table are premium." There, artists and writers mixed with those members of society who were interested in meeting fascinating people outside of their usual circle.

Not only did the party and others like it keep Chanel's name in the society pages of the newspaper, but she also had other ways of getting her name out in public. For example, she made it a habit to give her clothing for free to notable women who could be counted on to tell their friends, when asked what they were wearing, "It's Chanel."

And to ensure that there was a constant interest in her fashion, Chanel worked tirelessly, turning out new creations at a breathtaking pace. Madsen quotes Princess Marthe Bibesco, who proudly wore a wardrobe designed by Chanel for her travel by airplane, as commenting:

> What's trendy now and what's no longer smart are the two absolutes of her power. Her eyes are alert, her little head, her step are decisive. She doesn't talk much. "She came from nothing," her friends say. "Her grandmother was a shepherd, her mother from Auvergne." Yes, but it's in Paris she made it.

With 3,000 people under her employ, the House of Chanel expanded its workspace, annexing 27, 29, and 31 rue Cambon. The shop in Deauville, which was still a see-and-be-seen resort town, was still doing well, but with the decline of the popularity of Biarritz, a new shop, also a huge success, was opened in Cannes.

But even with her tremendous success, her beautiful home filled with antiques, her celebrity-studded parties, there was still a part of her that remained the orphan girl raised by nuns. Every morning when she arrived at work, she left behind her the aroma of the harsh lye soap that her "aunts" had trained her to use. Known for her remarkable sense of smell, she loathed the natural aroma of a woman's body, and it was said by Axel Madsen that one of her favorite quotes was "A woman who doesn't wear perfume has no future."

In light of that, it should perhaps not be surprising that she turned her attention to the possibility of creating a perfume of her own. Other designers had done so as well but had kept their creations within what had always been popular—straightforward floral scents.

But Chanel wanted something different. She turned to Ernest Beaux, the owner of a laboratory in Grasse, to help her find something new in the world of women's fragrance. According to Madsen, she told Beaux in no uncertain terms that

> I don't want hints of roses, of lilies of the valley. I want a perfume that is composed. It's a paradox. On a woman a natural flower scent smells artificial. Perhaps a natural perfume must be created artificially.

Beaux was startled by Chanel's sensitivity to smell. She told him that if somebody offered her a flower, not only could she smell the flower, but she could also smell the hands that picked them.

But making perfume requires more than just having a sensitive nose; it is a chemical process. For example, benzyl acetate is a product made from coal tar that smells like jasmine, but it cannot work as a replacement for jasmine extract, which is taken from the Spanish jasmine flower in a laborious and extremely expensive process. However, if one mixes benzyl acetate *with* jasmine extract, the end result is a perfume that does not quickly fade.

Chanel spent days away from her Paris salon to work alongside Beaux in his Grasse laboratory, sniffing, smelling, and categorizing aromas. If, for example, Beaux pointed out that the scent of one magnolia extract had an underlying hint of rot, of mushrooms, she would add, as quoted by Madsen, "That smells like leaf mold, of wet grass, something refreshing. It will help soften the scent of the tuberose."

Finally, Beaux settled on seven or eight samples to present to Chanel. She slowly went down the line, comparing one to the other, sniffing, contemplating, and contrasting the aromas. Finally she made her choice—the fifth sample was her final selection.

The perfume would be called simply "Chanel No. 5." It was the first time that a perfume was named after the designer and the first

With her growing fame came important connections. Here, Chanel hunts for boar with future British prime minister Winston Churchill and his son, Randolph.

time that a perfume was given a number and not a flowery name to go along with a flowery scent. And, in another break from tradition, Chanel designed the simple, modernistic, square, almost pharmaceutical bottle, which was so different from the ornately decorative bottles that had always been the desired look.

Now, the only question was how to market it. It would be expensive to make, very expensive indeed. The price of jasmine, Beaux told Chanel (as quoted by Madsen), contributed to the cost. "In that case, put even more jasmine in it," she said. "I want to make it the world's most expensive perfume."

That would be the perfume's niche, the way to market it, by making it something that appealed to a very select upper-end clientele. Chanel returned to Paris armed with small sample bottles of the perfume, which she then offered to only her best clients. The dressing rooms in her boutiques were sprayed with the scent. When customers began to ask where they could get more of the perfume, she would tell them that she wasn't in the perfume business and that it had just been a little gift for some of her best clients. She would then, according to Madsen, slyly add, "You think I should have it made and sell it? You mean you really like *my* perfume?"

The gambit worked. Because it was unavailable, even to those with money, her clients began demanding that she start making her perfume. Within a few weeks, bottles of Chanel No. 5 began reaching Gabrielle's shops in rue Cambon and her boutiques in Deauville, Biarritz, and Cannes. It was an immediate success. Chanel's great friend Misia, quoted by Axel Madsen, would later remark, "The success was beyond anything we could have imagined. It was like a winning lottery ticket."

Chanel No. 5 was so successful that it began to be sold by shops other than Chanel's. Years earlier, a young Coco had purchased straw boaters from Paris's largest department store, Galeries Lafayette, which she had then trimmed and decorated and which had been the start of her career. Now, the owner of that very same store wanted to carry Chanel No. 5. It must have given her a great sense of satisfaction, a clear demonstration of just how far she had come.

There was one problem, though. There was no way that Ernest Beaux's laboratory could produce enough Chanel No. 5 to meet the demand. But the owner of Galeries Lafayette, Théophile Bader, had two friends whom he thought could help. They were brothers, Pierre and Paul Wertheimer, from a wealthy Jewish family and the owners of Les parfumeries Bourjois, France's largest cosmetics and fragrance company. The association between Chanel and the Wertheimers would continue for the rest of their lives.

While Chanel was not averse to making money from Chanel No. 5, she did not want to get involved in the perfume end of the business, preferring to concentrate on fashion. She made a simple deal with the Wertheimers. She agreed to allow them to produce

I hate people touching me, rather as cats do. I walk straight along the path I have plotted for myself, even when it bores me; I am its slave, because I have chosen it freely. Being as tough as steel, I have never missed a day's work, and I've never been ill; I avoided various famous doctors who forecast different deadly diseases that I have failed to treat. Since the age of thirteen, I have no longer contemplated suicide.

I have made dresses, I could easily have done something else. It was an accident. I didn't like dresses, but I liked work. I have sacrificed everything to it, even love. Work has consumed my life.

—*from* Chanel and Her World: Friends, Fashion, and Fame
by Edmonde Charles-Roux

and distribute her perfumes, and in exchange, she would receive 10 percent of the profits.

To protect herself and her name, the new company could only sell products under the name "Chanel" that were considered to be a part of the perfume business. In addition, it was written into the contract that Les parfums Chanel could only sell top-quality products, since selling inferior products could hurt the Chanel name when it came to fashion. These stipulations would become a strong point of legal contention in the years to come.

But that would be in the future. Now, at the age of 40, she was the designer whose name symbolized her era. She had created a perfume that to this day remains so popular that it has been estimated that one bottle is sold worldwide every 55 seconds; one so popular that from its sales alone, Chanel earned financial independence for the rest of her life. She was, however, about to meet a man who would tempt her to give it all up, in order to become a member of royalty.

7

At Her Peak

His name was Hugh Richard Arthur Grosvenor. His mother, as well as future British prime minister Winston Churchill, called him "Benny," but his friends called him "Bender" or "Bendor," probably derived from the name of one his grandfather's most valuable horses. To the world at large, he was known as the second Duke of Westminster.

He was, in the words of Axel Madsen, "among the very fortunate in worldly standing and wealth, a man who owned vast tracts of choice London real estate . . . and shot, hunted, played polo, and cruised the world aboard his own pleasure boats." British playwright Noel Coward, as quoted by Madsen, said he was a "floridly handsome man, who, had he lived in an earlier age, would undoubtedly have glittered with rhinestones from head to foot."

He was a man who was easily pleased and just as easily bored, a man who could be charming when he wanted and rude if he didn't; a man who could have anyone and anything he wanted. And after meeting her on a yacht in Monte Carlo over the 1922–1923 Christmas and New Year's holidays, he wanted Gabrielle Chanel.

He took her gambling. He filled her hotel suite with flowers, and then filled her house in Paris with flowers after she returned home. He came to her house in the company of the Prince of Wales. He sent her fruits and flowers from his hothouses, and Scottish salmons from his streams. Still, Chanel hesitated.

There were a number of reasons. The main reason, of course, as it always was with Chanel, was her work. The House of Chanel was her life, and nothing else was or ever could be quite as important. Chanel also had her friends, most of them artists and writers like Cocteau, Picasso, and Maurice Sachs, friends with whom Bender did not quite fit in. Her great friend Misia did not look kindly upon the duke either, but that in itself was enough to send Chanel in the opposite direction; accepting an invitation to attend a shipboard dinner with 100 other people on his yacht, *The Flying Cloud*, docked in Bayonne harbor, near Biarritz.

When all the guests, with the exception of Coco, left the party the ship raised anchor. Bender and Chanel were left alone as the ship traveled along the coast, accompanied by just a crew of 40 and the orchestra the duke had hired for the occasion. It didn't take long before gossip columns in Britain and in the United States began predicting that Chanel would soon become the third Duchess of Westminster.

Chanel became more and more a part of Bender's life, assuming the role of mistress of his main residence, Eaton Hall. The life of British nobility was a new one for her, and for someone who lived for the cleanliness instilled in her by the nuns, it was an admirable existence. Of course, this was just the duke's main residence. He also had an estate in the Scottish highlands, a home in London, a hunting lodge in France's La forêt des Landes (Landes forest), as well as a château close to Deauville. But much to

Hugh Richard Arthur Grosvenor (*above*) was called "Bender" by his friends. Bender hurt Chanel with his infidelities, and she turned to her work as her first priority.

Chanel's dismay, Bender's favorite place to be was on one of his numerous ships. Although she hated sailing, she did her best to enjoy it for the duke's sake, and he was highly impressed by her courage during even the roughest of seas.

In fact, Chanel did whatever she could to make the relationship work. On one memorable occasion, Bender arranged a hunt for wild boars at his hunting lodge in La forêt des Landes. When one of the other hunter's shots sent a tree limb crashing down on Chanel, cutting her lower lip badly, the only available doctor was a veterinarian, who stitched up the cut as best he could before sending her home on the night train to Paris. She made the trip accompanied by her maid, as well as a monkey and parrot she had bought as gifts for the duke.

That night in her sleeping car, the monkey and bird began to go after each other. The monkey hid behind Chanel's skirts while the maid tried but failed to throw a towel over the parrot to calm it down. Coco later joked that was the event that caused her first real breakdown.

But although she could put up with a lot, one thing she would not tolerate was Bender's unfaithfulness. On one occasion, Bender invited an attractive young interior decorator to accompany them on a Mediterranean cruise. Chanel was furious when she found out, and the very next morning, the ship made an unscheduled landing to allow the decorator to disembark. Bender accompanied her onshore and returned to the ship bearing an expensive string of pearls as a peace offering.

According to lifelong friend Serge Lifar, it wasn't enough.

Proud and arrogant, Chanel couldn't stand being less than the one and only woman in Westminster's life. When the duke offered her the necklace, which was worth a fortune, Coco, in a gesture of superb defiance, let the pearls slide from her hand into the ocean.

(Madsen, *Chanel: A Woman of Her Own*)

And of course, being a "liberated" woman of the 1920s, she was pleased to show the duke that if he could have relationships with women other than her, she could see other men as well. One in particular, the married poet Pierre Reverdy, spent a great deal of time at her town house in rue du Faubourg Saint-Honoré. Reverdy wasn't attractive, and he certainly wasn't rich, but he had a mystical quality—the air of a poet—that drew Chanel to him. Still, throughout this period, the Duke of Westminster was her primary relationship.

It was, though, just a relationship. Her life was in her work, in the House of Chanel. And, just as during her "Slavic period," when her fashions reflected her interest in all things Russian, her relationship with Bender also influenced her designs. She began to introduce the look of the British aristocracy into women's fashion: blazers, vests, and cardigans based on traditional Scottish designs, shirts with cuff links, and what became her famous use of tweed were all inspired by her visits to the duke in Britain.

Her influences during this period did not come exclusively from the British aristocracy. Other, "humbler" forms of menswear such as sailor suits, berets, the neckerchiefs worn by stonemasons, and mechanics' dungarees were all transformed by her from simple men's workwear into women's high fashion.

It is safe to say, though, and cannot be emphasized enough, that Chanel was not a "designer" in the strictest sense of the word. She did not sketch, she did not "design" her clothes. She simply took basic designs and then elaborated on them, always using a real woman rather than a mannequin as her "canvas." Her genius was in the details, in the lines of the clothing, in the way it moved and made a woman look beautiful without overwhelming her. And as the mid-1920s began, Chanel was entering one of her peak periods of prestige and influence.

THE ART OF SIMPLICITY

Paris in 1925 saw an explosion of arts of all kinds—music, theater, and painting. But topping them all was L'Exposition internationale des Arts décoratifs et industriels modernes (The International

Exposition of Modern Industrial and Decorative Arts), a World's Fair of the arts held in Paris that year.

The fair introduced to France and to the world the term *art deco* (in French, "art déco," an abbreviation from the title of the exposition). This style, which was both new and functional, was streamlined, with sleek lines inspired by the modernism of the 1920s. Gone were curves, gone were the excesses of the previous style of art nouveau. In its place were straight lines, with the words *easy* and practical being key. Decoration for decoration's sake was out; utility and functionality were in. It was a look and style that Coco Chanel understood all too well. It was her time to shine.

TWO ICONIC LOOKS

Within the next two years, Gabrielle Chanel presented to the world the two items of clothing for which she is still best known: the Chanel suit and the little black dress.

The first to be introduced was the Chanel suit. Made up of a collarless cardigan jacket, with long, tightly fitted sleeves and a simple trim of braid worn over an elegant graceful skirt, it became one of the most popular looks in the history of fashion. It is a look that has been copied in every fabric and price range imaginable, more than "any other single garment designed by a couturier," according to Axel Madsen.

The other major design of the late 1920s was the fabled "little black dress," introduced in 1926. And while this dress may now hang in the closet of women worldwide, it was, for its time, revolutionary. Before Chanel, black had been seen as the color of mourning, a sign of bereavement. Coco turned it into a color of classic elegance, of understated simplicity.

How she arrived at the concept is another story shrouded in mystery. In one account, she was attending a gala opening at the opera and, while leaning over the railing of her box, witnessed a parade of women in the full regalia of Poiret designs, festooned with beads, feathers, and far too much material. Some say that

Coco on Broadway

It is a measure of the remarkable fame that Gabrielle Chanel achieved in her lifetime that as early as 1962, Broadway producers were at her doorstep, pleading with her to allow them to turn her story into a musical.

For years, Chanel was reluctant to say "yes." Finally though, in 1966, when two of the biggest names on Broadway, André Previn and Alan Jay Lerner, were brought in to compose the score, Coco gave in.

But it took a star to play a star. Film legend Katharine Hepburn (whom Chanel had met briefly during her 1933 trip to Hollywood), who had never performed in a musical before, was persuaded to take on the role.

Given Hepburn's age at the time (she was 60 years old in 1967), it was agreed that the show would focus on Chanel's 1954 come-back. After almost a year of rehearsals, *Coco* opened on Broadway on December 27, 1969. The show itself got lukewarm reviews, but for Hepburn, who really couldn't sing, it was a personal triumph, earning her rave notices and a Tony Award nomination.

But the show's true star, Gabrielle "Coco" Chanel, was unable to attend the Broadway premiere of her life story. One week before she was scheduled to leave for New York, she suffered a mild stroke. Chanel, who had been so reluctant to see her life story put on stage, was never able to attend a performance.

inspired her to go in the opposite direction, to a simple, black dress of perfect cut and design. In another version, it was her lingering love for Boy Capel that was her inspiration. "I'm going to put the whole world in mourning for him," was her stated reason for the dress, as quoted by Axel Madsen.

But whatever inspired her to design the dress, the idea was inspired. The dress, stripped of all sense of sculpture or ornament, a true art deco design, made headlines. There were daytime versions made from wool or marocain (a crepe fabric) and evening versions made from satin, satin-backed crepe, and printed and cut velvet. The evening dresses were set apart through the use of jeweled and rhinestone-studded belts and eyelets.

It was a look, a style, that women everywhere could use; one that they could dress up or dress down according to their own desires. And, perhaps more importantly, it was a dress designed by a woman for women. Previously, male designers had created dresses that men enjoyed looking at, dresses that emphasized a woman's breasts and derriere. Now, women could dress in a style that pleased *themselves*, in a simple yet beautiful dress that moved and allowed them to move, that made simplicity elegant, and made elegance simple.

Not surprisingly perhaps, male fashion journalists were aghast. "No more bosom, no more stomach, no more rump," said one quoted by Edmonde Charles-Roux. Designer Paul Poiret was driven to make his famous remark, also cited by Charles-Roux, "What has Chanel invented? De luxe poverty. Formerly women were architectural, like the prows of ships, and very beautiful. Now they resemble little undernourished telegraph clerks."

There was a bigger question. Critics questioned whether women would want to wear the same dress that was also being worn by hordes of *other* women. *Vogue* featured the caption "Here is a Ford signed 'Chanel'" next to a drawing of the dress, implying that, like a Ford car, the dress was being designed for the masses. Would it sell?

It did. By putting the Chanel name on it, just by the act of having women all over the world wearing the dress, it became a guarantee of quality. Fashion, which had for so many years meant a one-of-a-kind look, now entered the age of standardization. The influence of Chanel had once again changed the way women thought about clothing, about fashion, about their look.

Indeed, as *Vogue* pointed out in an unsigned editorial, people bought cars that were identical to everybody else's because they

One of Chanel's most enduring creations was the "little black dress," one example of which is shown above. The details of the little black dress have evolved throughout the years, but the essential concept has made it a classic.

believed that sameness was a guarantee of quality. With Chanel's clothing, it was not so much that the clothing made the woman, but with its simple and elegant design, the woman made the clothing, as quoted by Madsen:

> But the world as a whole now looks pretty much alike to an outsider, as its civilized inhabitants prance along in the same shaped trouserings and slip-on frocks. Of course, the shapes inside these garments differ, thank goodness, and there is still an appearance and carriage called "queenly," a behavior known as "princely," and a loveliness likened to that of a "princess in a fairytale."

Consider for a moment, the everyday clothing in schools—probably jeans and T-shirts. Now, consider how great one person may look in that clothing compared to another. It's not the clothing that makes them look good—it's how they wear the clothing, their attitude, and the way it fits. It's the same with the Chanel little black dress. It may be uniform, and it may be elegant and stylish, but its look varies depending on the woman wearing it.

SHOULD SHE MARRY?

As her fashions grew in popularity and influence, so did her empire. In 1927, Chanel opened a boutique in London in the heart of the fashionable Mayfair district. There, her sports clothes (by which she meant "clothes for *watching* sports in," as described by Madsen) were purchased by many of Britain's elite: the wife of the future king of England, the Duchess of York, and other featured players in the society and gossip pages.

British *Vogue* raved about her clothes:

> Looks designed for sports graduate to country day-dressing and then arrive in town, and Chanel's country tweeds have just completed the course. She pins a white pique gardenia to the neck. . . . She initiates fake jewelry, to be worn everywhere, even on the beach.

Although her fashions were wholly original and revolutionized women's fashion, Chanel's designs have endured because they allow the wearer to shine through. Chanel's theory that the person should wear the clothes, not the other way around, has been the foundation of modern fashion.

But what truly fascinated the British press even more than her fashions was her personal life: Was she or wasn't she, they breathlessly speculated, going to marry the Duke of Westminster?

The question lingered, unanswered, between Chanel and the duke for years. There were problems. Chanel was not willing to give up her career, which was the center of her life. There was the constant worry of being embarrassed by her brothers, one of whom, Alphonse, worked behind the counter of a cigarette store; the other of whom, Lucien, worked a shoe stall. Neither of them were suitable siblings for the possible next Duchess of Westminster.

That problem was easily taken care of—a sizable amount of money to both was enough to make them disappear from sight. There was one problem, however, that all the money in the world couldn't fix. Chanel was now 42 years old, and whoever married Bender had the responsibility to provide him with an heir to assume his title after he was gone. Coco's childbearing days were rapidly ending.

She did what she could. She saw doctors. She visited women who gave advice on how to become pregnant. She spent a fortune on a 5-acre (2-hectare) property overlooking the Mediterranean, then spent three times that amount rebuilding it to her liking, all in the hopes that a romantic setting would help her in her quest to bear Bender's child. Visitors to the estate included such luminaries as Winston Churchill and his wife. "La Pausa was the most comfortable, relaxing place I have ever stayed," Axel Madsen quotes Bettina Ballard as having said.

ELEMENTS OF STYLE

Where then does the couturier's genius lie? The genius is in anticipating. More than a great statesman, the great couturier is a man who has the future in his mind. His genius is to invent summer dresses in the winter, and vice versa. At a time when his customers are basking in the burning sun, he is thinking of ice and of hoar frost.

—*from* Chanel and Her World: Friends, Fashion, and Fame
by Edmonde Charles-Roux

Unfortunately, despite the romantic, relaxing atmosphere, Chanel did not become pregnant. She would soon, though, have far bigger things to worry about. She was now 46 years old, and the world was about to go through bigger changes than even Coco Chanel could have imagined.

8

The War Years

On Tuesday, October 29, 1929, the U.S. stock market crashed, sending the nation's economy into a tailspin that led to the Great Depression, leaving millions of people out of work and the nation on the brink of collapse. And while the events in the United States ultimately led to worldwide depression, it took a full year for the effects to be felt in Europe.

The year 1930 was one of Chanel's biggest ever. She designed gowns for some of Paris's best-known young women, all of whom had been invited to one of the grandest balls the city had ever seen, one for which the guests were commanded to come dressed, as quoted by Axel Madsen, "like somebody everybody knew." But by the following year, hard times had hit Europe as well, and, not surprisingly, it was the upper-end, luxury trades that got hit first.

Chanel's designs were the most expensive in Paris, and as the depression deepened and economic suffering became widespread, even the wealthy did not want to wear clothing that made them *look* rich. Chanel's clothing, which while expensive did not have the overdressed look that fit the stereotypical view of wealthy women, seemingly fit the times. And Chanel adjusted as necessary, introducing cotton as a fashion fabric in evening dresses. She even cut prices at her salons in half. But with rich Americans on the Riviera few and far between, and the rest of the European wealthy not willing to spend money on high fashion, Chanel was forced to lay off workers and look for other ways to extend her influence.

She wasn't hurting financially of course. Years of success had earned her far more money than she could ever hope to spend. But she was hurting in other ways. Her relationship with Bender was at an impasse. The two did have a loving relationship, but she wasn't willing to give up the House of Chanel, and it was, at that time, unacceptable for the Duchess of Westminster to also be a successful, independent businesswoman. And, there was still the lingering question of an heir.

It became too much, and the duke, who had never been particularly faithful to Coco, began to be seen more and more about town with Loelia Mary Ponsonby, daughter of first Baron Sysonby. The pair became engaged in the spring of 1930, and Bender brought his fiancée to meet Chanel. Years later, Madsen writes, Loelia recalled the somewhat tense meeting:

> Small, dark, and simian, Coco was the personification of her own fashion. She was wearing a dark blue suit and a white blouse with very light stockings (light stockings were one of her credos). Described in this way she sounds as if she looked like a high-school girl, but actually the effect was one of extreme sophistication. . . . When I saw her she was hung with every sort of necklace and bracelet, which rattled as she moved. . . . I perched, rather at a disadvantage, on a stool at her feet, feeling that I was

being looked over to see whether I was a suitable bride for her old admirer—and I very much doubted whether I, or my tweed suit, passed the test.

Conversation was uncomfortable. Trying to find something to say, Loelia told Chanel that several years before, a friend of her parents had given her a Chanel necklace as a Christmas present. Chanel pressed her to describe it and, after she finished, told Loelia in no uncertain terms that the necklace could not possibly have come from her, and even more, she would never have dreamed of having anything like that for sale in any of her boutiques.

Chanel also revolutionized jewelry, making it fashionable to wear an abundance of costume jewelry. Here, she models the look.

On February 20, 1930, Bender married Loelia. Winston Churchill was his best man. One year later, Gabrielle Chanel boarded the SS *Europe* bound for America, accompanied by her friend Misia. She had decided to accept an offer from Samuel Goldwyn to come to Hollywood, look around, and see if she might be interested in designing for films. Chanel herself had no expectations of staying or even liking Hollywood, telling the *New York Times*:

> It's just an invitation. I will see what the pictures have to offer me and what I have to offer the pictures. I will not make one dress. I have not brought my scissors with me. Later, perhaps, when I get back to Paris, I will create and design gowns.

Others, though, were more optimistic about her possible impact on Hollywood and American design. As Madsen writes, Bergdorf Goodman's Comtesse de Forceville commented:

> *They are crazy over her creations. Chanel will never be short of ideas. Over the past ten, fifteen years the fashions that count have been conceived by her. It'll be a triumphant success and it will be a great plus for the cinema.*

She met many Hollywood greats, including director Erich von Stroheim, who, according to Axel Madsen, kissed her hand and asked, "You are . . . a seamstress, I believe?" She also met rising star Katharine Hepburn, who, nearly 40 years later, would play the role of Gabrielle Chanel on Broadway.

Goldwyn was seemingly more interested in the publicity he received from bringing Coco Chanel to Hollywood than in actually using her services. For her part, Chanel took a strong dislike to Hollywood and movie stars. She designed a few dresses for dancer Charlotte Greenwood for the film *Palmy Days*, agreed to design costumes for the upcoming *Tonight or Never* starring film great Gloria Swanson, and got on the next train back to New York City.

There, she met (and charmed) the editors of the nation's most powerful fashion magazines, *Harper's Bazaar* and *Vogue*. But for Chanel, the most eye-opening aspect of her 1933 visit was a trip to Klein's discount clothing shop. There, dresses similar to the expensive Chanel dresses sold on Fifth Avenue were on sale for just a few dollars: inexpensive copies made from cheaper materials. While other designers would be furious that their work was being "stolen" in that manner, Chanel was flattered. To her, the fact that people from all walks of life wanted to wear her clothes, even in a cheap copy, was proof of her success.

BACK TO PARIS

She returned to a Paris still in the depths of the depression, a city still with little interest in haute couture. But ironically, there *was* an interest in expensive jewelry in part as an investment, an interest that Chanel was ready to capitalize upon.

Through the 1920s, Chanel had popularized relatively inexpensive costume jewelry and artificial pearls, turning them into status symbols. Now she took the other tack, according to Madsen, promoting a mix of the real and the artificial:

> A woman should mix fake and real. To ask a woman to wear real jewelry only is like asking her to cover herself with real flowers instead of flowery silk prints. She'd look faded in a few hours.
>
> I love fakes because I find such jewelry provocative, and I find it disgraceful to walk around with millions around your neck just because you're rich. The point of jewelry isn't to make a woman look rich but to adorn her; not the same thing.

She was now at the peak of her power and influence as a designer, but as in everything else, nobody stays at the top forever. There were new designers on the scene ready to rival her as the leader of French fashion. One such designer was Elsa Schiaparelli.

Her designs were the polar opposite of Chanel's. Whereas Chanel stood for classic simplicity, Schiaparelli stood for baroque excess. Whereas Chanel aimed to liberate women from the need to overdress, Schiaparelli's clothing personified luxury—they looked expensive in ways that Chanel's clothing did not. Chanel boasted that her designs were copied round the world; Schiaparelli was proud of her uniqueness. "What I create is inimitable," she is quoted as saying by Axel Madsen.

Schiaparelli designed clothing for the brave, for women who wanted to stand out from the crowd. She built her collections around themes designed for fantasy: circuses, music, butterflies. Her fashion made a huge splash among those tired of dressing to suit the economic times: Film star Greta Garbo, the Duchess of Windsor, as well as Italian dictator Benito Mussolini's assorted girlfriends were among her best-known customers.

Besides new rivals, there were growing problems with her business partners, the Wertheimers. Chanel had begun to regret the deal she had made, giving them 90 percent of Chanel No. 5. For while sales of the world's number one perfume had made her rich, they had made the Wertheimers even richer.

Her chance for revenge arrived in 1934, with the arrival on store shelves of Chanel cleansing cream, brought out by the Wertheimers without any prior approval from Coco herself. And while the contract she had signed had given the corporation headed by the Wertheimers the right to sell "under the name Chanel, all perfumes, beauty products, soaps, etc.," it also restricted such sales, according to Madsen, "to objects usually sold in the perfume business."

It boiled down to one simple question: Is a cleansing cream a perfume product or a beauty product? Chanel filed suit against the Wertheimers, trying to deny them the use of her name on a cleansing cream. The Wertheimers responded that cleansing creams were, in fact, part of the perfume business. The court battle was on, the first round of which would last for five years.

Elsa Schiaparelli

Perhaps the only real rival to Gabrielle Chanel for fashion supremacy during the period between World War I and World War II was Italian fashion designer Elsa Schiaparelli.

Schiaparelli (September 10, 1890–November 13, 1973) was the daughter of a scholar and curator of medieval manuscripts and a Neapolitan aristocrat. She studied philosophy at the University of Rome, but after publishing a book of poems with strong sexual content, her parents sent her to live in a convent until, after a hunger strike, she was allowed to leave to accept a job as a nanny in London.

There, she quickly immersed herself in a life of art and design, visiting museums and attending lectures, even marrying one of her lecturers, Count William de Wendt de Kerlor. The couple moved to New York in 1921, where she quickly embraced the modernism of the city. After her husband abandoned her, Schiaparelli became friends with Gaby Picabia, the former wife of an artist and owner of a fashionable women's clothing store, and the photographer Man Ray. When Gaby and Man Ray moved to Paris, Schiaparelli went with them.

IRIBE

In the meantime, there was a new man in her life, one whom Chanel called the most complicated man she had ever known. Paul Iribe was an artist and designer, a cartoonist, an illustrator, a furniture designer, an artistic director for such Hollywood films as *The Affairs of Anatol*, *The Ten Commandments*, and *King of Kings*. He was also a jewelry designer whose wife, heiress Maybelle Hogan, got him commissions to design jewelry for both Cartier and Chanel.

Iribe, although still married to Hogan, had a charm, wit, and self-confidence that allowed him to win over Chanel. For a year,

It was there that she began designing her own clothes, launching a collection of knitwear in 1927 featuring sweaters with surrealist images. One sweater in particular, a design that made it look as though the wearer had a scarf wrapped around her neck, earned her her first major recognition.

She quickly moved into sportswear and added eveningwear to her collection in 1931. Schiaparelli is known for her use of graphic knitwear with colorful patterns; prints of body parts, food, and other unusual themes; brightly colored zippers; and elaborate buttons in the shape of peanuts, bees, and even ram heads. She collaborated with many contemporary artists, including Salvador Dali and Jean Cocteau, to design many of her more elaborate creations. Examples include a jacket embroidered with the figure of a woman with her hand caressing the waist of the wearer, with long blond hair flowing down one sleeve. A dress featuring large, hand-painted lobsters. A dress printed with designs that made the dress look like it was covered with rips and tears. A skeleton dress with quilting added to simulate ribs, a spine, and leg bones. And, a hat shaped like a woman's high-heeled shoe.

But despite her unique view of fashion, Schiaparelli was unable to adapt to the changes brought about by World War II, and she was forced to close her business in 1954. Ironically, that was the very year that Gabrielle Chanel made her triumphant comeback.

they managed to keep their relationship a secret, but eventually Maybelle learned of the affair, moved out of their apartment, and left for America with their two children.

Chanel began to rely more and more on Iribe, even giving him power of attorney to preside over the board meeting of Les parfums Chanel. There, he was outmaneuvered by the Wertheimers, who arranged for the board members to vote him out, after which they reorganized the company, replaced Chanel as president, and gradually absorbed the business into the Wertheimer Company, leaving Chanel angrily plotting new ways to avenge herself against the Wertheimers.

But although she was losing her battles with the Wertheimers, her clothing was still winning over the public and critics alike. Her 1934 look, open-necked white shirts worn underneath artificial silk dresses, won raves from British *Vogue*, especially in contrast with Schiaparelli's 1934 designs, which included wearing a felt sock as a hat.

Even so, and even with the knowledge that *Vogue* had done a major story on her and her work, including what would become an iconic photograph of her by the young photographer Horst, Chanel was still angry at the publicity Condé Nast (the publisher of *Vogue*) was giving to her archrival, Elsa Schiaparelli. Here, for the first time in years, was a designer who truly competed with Chanel for the attention of the fashion world. After returning from her summer-long break in Roquebrune, as quoted by Madsen, she swore that she would come back to "deal a death blow to 'that Italian.'"

The summer turned to tragedy. One bright morning, Chanel and Iribe were playing tennis. Halfway through the first set, Iribe fell to the ground after suffering a massive heart attack. At the age of 52, Paul Iribe, the man many believed Chanel would marry, was dead.

ANOTHER PERIOD OF MOURNING

Once again, Chanel was alone. She remained at Roquebrune in mourning, letting her staff run her businesses until her return to Paris in October. It was time to unveil her fashion line for 1936, and her rivalry with Schiaparelli was heating up even more.

Chanel kept to her classic lines, offering a variation on her previous looks: tweed suits this year, worn over open-necked white shirts. In contrast, Schiaparelli's headline-making look, designed in conjunction with surreal artist Salvador Dali, was something completely new: an evening dress whose skirt was printed with a life-size lobster, along with green splotches to represent parsley. When Wallis Simpson, the Duchess of Windsor, was photographed by Cecil Beaton wearing the dress, it was a major victory for Schiaparelli.

As biographer Axel Madsen points out, Chanel and Schiaparelli were in the process of creating two very different schools of fashion.

> Gabrielle was now the designer for hesitant, unassertive women. Those who were reserved and feared bad taste more than anything else wore Chanel; cheeky, self-assured, and alluring women had fun with Schiaparelli's red eyelashes, black gloves with scarlet fingernails, coarse hairnets anchoring pancake hats, light blue satin pants showing under the lifted hem of a black evening dress.

Within three years, though, the fight for influence between Chanel and Schiaparelli would pale in significance to the fight being fought around the world.

CHANGES IN THE AIR

Political change was happening all over Europe throughout the 1930s. In Germany, Adolf Hitler had taken power, while in Italy, Benito Mussolini had done the same; both heading fascist governments determined to rule Europe and the rest of the world.

In France in 1936, the Front populaire (Popular Front) received 85 percent of the vote, bringing a leftist coalition to power on the promise of enacting much-needed social and economic reforms. Encouraged by this development, workers throughout the nation went on strike, taking over factories and workplaces and demanding paid vacations, family support, unemployment insurance, and a guaranteed 40-hour workweek. Among the strikers were the 3,000 employees of the House of Chanel.

The newly elected president of France, Léon Blum, met with labor leaders and representatives of the leading employers' association to make a deal, known as the Matignon agreements. In exchange for the workers ending their strikes, they would receive raises ranging from 7 to 15 percent, the right to organize and form unions, a guaranteed 40-hour workweek, and two weeks of paid vacation per year. Chanel was appalled.

Chanel felt that "her girls" were getting paid quite enough as it was, and if they weren't, well, there were always men available who could help them. Her initial response to the strike was to fire 300 women, but when they refused to leave the premises of her workshops and boutiques, tensions between Chanel and her workers continued to mount.

At first she simply refused to negotiate. But as time passed, and the realization grew that if she didn't come to an agreement soon she would not be able to compete with Schiaparelli, who *had* reached an agreement with her workers, Chanel had no choice but to give in to her workers' demands. With word reaching her that Schiaparelli's newest creations featured evening coats with

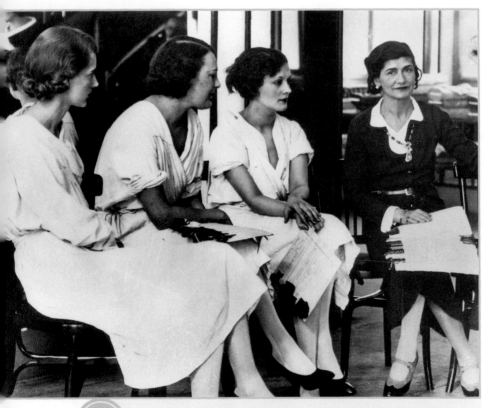

Chanel sits with employees from her Paris shop in 1936. Although she felt she paid the employees quite well, they went on strike.

embroidered Cocteau drawings, and scarves and hats illustrated with reprinted news stories about Elsa herself, Chanel knew she would have her work cut out for her.

But for the next few years, her heart didn't seem to be in it. She brought out new designs—including a gold lamé evening dress and a chopped jacket in 1938; and short, fitted jackets and big, pocketed skirts in 1939—but the battle with her workers, her lone-liness, and years of hard work were finally catching up with her.

War tensions were mounting throughout Europe. On August 26, 1939, a general mobilization was called for France, and more than a million men were called up. On September 1, 1939, German troops invaded Poland. The next day, Britain and France, determined to stop Hitler's aggression, declared war on Germany. Just three weeks later, Gabrielle Chanel announced that she was closing the House of Chanel and laying off her entire staff for the duration of the war.

WHY DID SHE DO IT?

Rumors abounded as to why she did it. Some thought that it was her ultimate act of revenge against her workers for their strike in 1936. Others felt that she believed that Schiaparelli had beat her in the fight for fashion dominance and that she just wanted to walk away gracefully. Chanel herself never gave a completely satisfying answer to the question of why she closed up shop.

For months, it seemed that nothing was going to happen in France, as the fighting remained largely limited to Poland. But in April 1940, German troops attacked Denmark and Norway, air-fields in northern France were hit by the German Luftwaffe, and German tanks crossed the borders of Holland and Belgium and within days were moving into France itself.

By June 4, the outskirts of Paris were under attack, and a mas-sive movement out of the city began. Chanel, now living at L'hôtel Ritz, packed her bags, paid her bills two months in advance, and, accompanied only by her driver, joined the millions fleeing the Nazi invasion. On June 21, an armistice was signed between Germany and France. By the end of August 1940, Chanel had returned to Paris and reinstalled herself in the Ritz, now occupied by German military officers. She would remain there throughout the war.

LIVING WITH THE GERMANS

Many of her friends, including Misia, were appalled that she would even consider living in the Ritz among Germans who were, after all, the enemy. Chanel pointed out that all hotels would eventually be occupied, so what did it matter where she lived?

Living under German occupation was a difficult, tragic time for all involved. A brave few continued to resist the Nazis. Others just lay low, hoping to stay out of trouble. Still others, known as collaborators (although they themselves thought they were just being practical and realistic), worked and lived with the Nazi occupiers, trying to continue living their lives in as normal a way as possible.

When Chanel's nephew, André Palasse, was not among the prisoners of war released by the Germans upon the signing of the armistice, she approached a dashing German she had often seen at the Ritz in the company of Foreign Minister Joachim von Ribbentrop for help. His name was Hans Gunther von Dincklage. He spoke French fluently, and while he wasn't able to help personally, he did put Chanel in touch with a friend of his, Captain Theodor Momm.

Momm's task in occupied France was to rebuild the French textile industry and gear its efforts toward assisting the German war machine. Given this, it was easy for Momm, after reopening a textile mill in the Paris suburb of Saint-Quentin, to convince authorities that the nephew of the great Gabrielle Chanel would be the perfect man to run the plant.

Chanel's nephew was released and sent to Paris to manage the textile mill, and Chanel, now 58 years old, began a relationship with von Dincklage, known as Spatz, who was 12 years younger. The couple kept a low profile during the war years, not being seen in fashionable restaurants or clubs. In her mind, Chanel was doing what she had to do to get by, to survive the war. Among friends,

Chanel struck up a relationship with Hans Gunther von Dincklage, also known as Spatz, during the war. Here, the two are photographed in 1951.

according to Madsen, both she and Spatz spoke out against the war, believing it to be "beneath contempt, vulgar, and second-rate."

But with the House of Chanel closed, she had a lot of free time on her hands. It wasn't until 1943 that she did any work at all, when she redid the costumes for Jean Cocteau's production of the Greek tragedy *Antigone*, by Sophocles. Much of her time was spent quietly at the Ritz returning to her first love: singing while accompanying herself on the piano.

She also busied herself in plotting against those she saw as her archenemies: the Wertheimer brothers. The German occupation of France gave her just the opportunity she needed. Under Nazi law, Jews were forbidden to engage in most business and professional activities. The Wertheimers were Jewish and had fled France early in the war, going through Spain, on to Portugal, and eventually ending up in the United States, leaving the company in the hands of a cousin, Raymond Bollack.

Chanel hoped to use this to her advantage to win back control of her perfume Chanel No. 5, her name, and the company Les parfums Chanel itself. She moved quickly, placing a spy, Georges Madoux, on the board, who was promptly elected the CEO. It seemed that Chanel was now poised to take control, but the Wertheimers were too fast for her.

Bollack stepped down, but not before finding a non-Jewish industrialist to become the public head of the company for legal purposes, while the Wertheimers, still in the United States, remained very much in charge. Papers were forged and produced to show the Germans that the company had been in non-Jewish hands for years. Once again, Chanel had lost. In the meantime, while she was not producing fashion, Chanel No. 5 was still being sold by Les parfums Chanel everywhere that was under German control. In addition, unbeknownst to her, it was also being sold in the United States by the Wertheimers themselves.

COULD SHE END THE WAR?

Beaten back once again by the Wertheimers, all Chanel could do was wait for the end of the war to come and for normal life to return to France. Spatz, whose true position with the Germans remains a mystery, knew by 1943 that the Germans had little chance to win the war. The only question, he felt, was when and how the war would end.

One day, while discussing what life would be like after the war and how it would end, Chanel turned to Spatz and said, according to Madsen, "You Germans don't know how to handle the English! I do!" Within months, Chanel, accompanied by her friend Vera Bate, was on a mission to Spain to meet with her longtime friend, British prime minister Winston Churchill, with a peace proposal from the Germans.

How did this happen? Chanel, now 60 years old, went to the man who had gotten her nephew released from a POW (prisoner of war) camp, Theodor Momm. They met in her drawing room at the Ritz. Chanel was certain that there must be high-ranking Germans who believed that with the United States in the war, Germany was destined to lose. She was also certain that Churchill, who knew all too well how the war was draining the resources of the British Empire, wanted to end the war as well.

She knew that Churchill would be pleased to receive her and was convinced that if she could just get her old friend Churchill to listen to her, the war could come to a rapid end. She is quoted by Madsen as saying, "Isn't it in everybody's interest to shorten the war, to save tens of thousands, perhaps hundreds of thousands of lives?"

It was called Operation Modellhut (named—in honor of Chanel—Operation "Fashion Hat"). It did not, however, work out as Chanel and her German handlers had hoped. Upon arriving in Madrid (and checking in to that city's Hotel Ritz), Chanel contacted British ambassador Samuel Hoare, telling him that she wished to meet with her old friend Winston. She also passed along a message to him from the man in charge of her mission, Major Walter Schellenberg of the SS (Schutzstaffel, a special Nazi police), that certain members of the German high command were ready to enter into secret talks to end the war.

Chanel never met with Churchill. She was informed by the ambassador that Churchill was gravely ill and wasn't meeting with anybody. The truth, though, which was revealed years later, was that Churchill was not even in Madrid! In reality, he was meeting with General Dwight D. Eisenhower at his headquarters in Tunisia. (And of course, there was a complete air of unreality regarding Chanel's proposal, which had not even been presented to Hitler. Hitler would never have entered into peace talks with anybody; until the war's end and his own suicide, he was certain that Germany would prevail.)

Chanel flew to Berlin to meet with Schellenberg. Although the exact dates remain uncertain, British intelligence believes that it took place in April 1944, just one year before the end of the war. What is not known is what she did there, how long she was there, and what she told Schellenberg.

Two months later, on June 6, 1944, Allied forces led by General Eisenhower landed on the French coast at Normandy—D-Day had begun. By July, American troops were just 56 miles (90 kilometers) outside of Paris. The Germans, along with their collaborators, made plans to flee Paris to disappear into Germany. Spatz begged Chanel to go with him to Switzerland, but Chanel decided to remain in Paris. Despite having had one of the enemy as her lover, despite her failed mission to Madrid and subsequent trip to Berlin, she was sure that she had nothing to fear.

On August 26, 1944, French resistance leader Charles de Gaulle entered Paris, watched by millions of cheering French men and women as he walked to La place de la Concorde, his mere presence proclaiming victory over the Germans. But within days, the arrests began, as anyone suspected of being a collaborator with the hated Germans was rounded up for questioning. Those accused could spend months in prison without trial; many women who had had "relations" with Germans had their heads shaved in public and were paraded down the street in utter humiliation.

Gabrielle Chanel was arrested in September 1944 and left the Ritz perfectly dressed, complete with gloves and a handbag. "Coco behaved like a queen, like Marie Antoinette being led to the scaffold," a witness later recalled, quoted by Madsen. "She left with the two Frenchmen who came to arrest her with her head high."

She was held for questioning for three hours and released. Why was she released so quickly when others who had done the same or less than her were sent to prison? British Foreign Office files suggest that it was because she knew information about Churchill that the British did not want to have revealed.

In exchange for her silence, no charges were ever filed against her. It was, however, still felt to be in her best interest to lie low until things blew over. She soon left France and settled in Switzerland, where she remained, in comfortable exile, until 1953.

9

The Return

There were a number of reasons why Chanel chose Switzerland for her base of operations during what became known as her years of oblivion.

There was her ongoing battle with the Wertheimers. When the brothers returned to Paris at the end of the war, she learned that while in America, they had formed a new corporation, Chanel, Inc., to manufacture Chanel No. 5 in America. They made a fortune—the perfume was sold in every armed forces PX around the world—but made a deposit of only $15,000 in royalties for Chanel herself in a Zurich account. She vowed, yet again, to get her revenge.

She started a new perfume line on her own, finding a perfumer in Switzerland to produce her new scent, which she labeled "Mademoiselle Chanel No. 5," and in 1946 began selling the fragrance in her boutique. The Wertheimers went to court, claiming that they owned the sole right to manufacture perfume using the name "Chanel." They won an immediate injunction, went to her rue Cambon boutique, and seized every bottle. Chanel immediately filed suit against the Wertheimers and left for Lausanne, Switzerland.

But there was more than perfume manufacturing that attracted her to Lausanne. Waiting for her there was her German boyfriend, Hans Gunther "Spatz" von Dincklage. The two reunited and reestablished their relationship, as Chanel continued to fight the Wertheimers in court, both in France and in the United States. It looked to be a long, knock-down legal battle, one that had the possibility of draining the resources of all involved.

It was the Wertheimers who "blinked" and asked for a settlement in 1947. The new agreement gave Chanel the right to produce and sell her perfume "Mademoiselle Chanel," as long as she no longer attached the "5" to it. Her royalties from the Wertheimer's American production of Chanel No. 5 were greatly increased (to well over $2 million in 2010 currency), and finally, Chanel would also receive royalties of 2 percent on all Chanel products manufactured and sold by the Wertheimers worldwide.

SITTING ON THE SIDELINES

There were occasional trips to France and one to New York in 1953, but for Chanel, the years 1947 to 1953 were spent quietly, doing little, in Switzerland. She was on the sidelines, watching as fashion trends such as the "New Look" came into being, as new designers such as Christian Dior, Balenciaga, and Rochas took their places in the spotlight, and old rivals such as Elsa Schiaparelli went into retirement.

But by 1950, her relationship with Spatz gradually came to an end, boredom began to set in, and rumors began to circulate that she was preparing to reopen the House of Chanel. To many in the fashion world, the idea was outlandish. With the rapid changes in

Just weeks after her death, more than 1,000 people crowded into Chanel's Paris salon to view her last collection.

fashion, she had become almost forgotten. Her classic suits, evening dresses, and jackets were seen as a relic of a long-ago past, one swept away by Dior, Givenchy, and a whole host of male designers who had come to the forefront since the war.

At the age of 70, Gabrielle Chanel reopened the House of Chanel in 1953, backed in large part by the Wertheimers, and presented her first fashion line in over a decade. She was convinced that women were already tired of the New Look, of the clinched waists, padded bras, and stiff jackets that seemed a step back from the relaxed elegance that Chanel had brought to fashion.

But instead, the Parisian press almost unanimously declared her time long gone; her clothing dated and passé. As writer Michel Déon wrote in an article published in *Les Nouvelles littéraries*:

> The French press were atrocious in their vulgarity, meanness and stupidity. They drubbed away at her age, assuring every-one that she had learned nothing in fifteen years of silence. We watched the mannequins file by in icy silence.

But while the French looked down at Chanel's creations, just three weeks later, the American response was one of elated cheers. *Life* magazine, in the introduction to a four-page article on her new line, declared that Chanel—"the name behind the most famous perfume in the world"—according to Madsen, had lost none of her skills as a designer.

> Her styles hark back to her best of the thirties—lace evening dresses that have plenty of elegant dash and easy-fitting suits that are refreshing after the "poured-on" look of some styles—and also feature such innovations as nylon.

Her dresses flew out of stores as women, not necessarily con-cerned with what the French press thought, found the classically simple Chanel silhouette refreshingly *modern*, as opposed to the rich sophistication of Dior and Balenciaga. As Axel Madsen points out, after six years of cinched-in waists and clothing built so that it could stand up on its own, simple and elegant clothing that once again allowed them to move *was*, in fact, new.

Even the French began to give her designs a second look. French *Vogue* featured on its cover model Marie-Hélène Arnaud, wearing, as quoted by Madsen, a Chanel "navy-blue jersey suit with squared shoulders, tucked crisp white blouse with a bow tie, sailor hat tipped to the back of her head, and her hands in the shirt pockets." Gabrielle Chanel, whose look gave women secu-rity and the knowledge that the clothing made them look good, was back.

A second collection served only to confirm what the public already knew: Gabrielle Chanel had reestablished herself at the top of the haute couture world. When asked to explain how she did it, her answer, according to Charles-Roux, was very simple: "A garment must be logical." And her clothing was always logical, looking good not only on the hanger, but on the woman wearing it. It was clothing that made sense and was simple, elegant, and refined. It was a look that was unmistakable—a look that said Chanel.

Other designers, such as Yves Saint Laurent, would have a smash success one year, a failure the next. But Chanel, her clothing, and her influence seemed timeless. An article in *Vogue* in March 1959 summed up her appeal and her influence:

> If fashion has taken a turn to the woman, no one can deny that much of the impetus for that turn stems from Coco Chanel—the fierce, wise, wonderful, and completely self-believing Chanel . . . . It is not that other Paris collections are like Chanel's. They are not. But the heady idea that a woman should be more important than her clothes, and that it takes superb design to keep her looking that way—this idea, which has been for almost forty years the fuel for the Chanel engine, has now permeated the fashion world.

Her clothing was worn by many of the world's most beautiful and influential women. Actresses, fashion stylistas, and everyday women everywhere wore Chanel. When U.S. first lady Jacqueline Kennedy accompanied her husband, President John F. Kennedy, to Dallas the day he was shot, she was wearing a pink Chanel suit. Coco Chanel's look was unmistakable, and it was everywhere.

And she worked hard to keep it so. Her look did not change that much from year to year, but it was constantly refined and updated without ever becoming the moment's trend. Whether it was her 1956 black suit with white lining and a white blouse, or

Christian Dior

The most influential designer of the period immediately following World War II, the creator of the "New Look," was Christian Dior.

Dior (January 21, 1905–October 24, 1957), heir to a fertilizer fortune, grew up wanting a life in fashion. He started early, selling fashion sketches outside of school for around 10 cents each. After graduating, his father gave him enough money to open a small art gallery, but after his family suffered enormous financial loses, he was forced to close the gallery.

Throughout the 1930s and into the 1940s, Dior worked for fashion designer Robert Piguet. After leaving the army in 1942, he joined the fashion house of Lucien Lelong, where, for the remainder of World War II, he helped to dress the wives of Nazi officers as well as those of leading French collaborators. On October 8, 1946, he left to open his own fashion house.

Although his first collection was actually called "Corolle" (after *corolla*, or "circlet of flower petals"), it was labeled "New Look" by Carmel Snow, the editor-in-chief of the leading fashion magazine *Harper's Bazaar*. Where the designs leading up to and during the war had been relatively severe, obviously military inspired, Dior's fashions were voluptuous, with rich, abundant fabrics draping women's bodies, once again made curvaceous with the use of tiny-waisted corsets and hip padding.

It was a revolt against everything that Chanel had stood for—once again women were being shaped to fit the dress, rather than the dress being shaped to fit the woman. But it was a brilliant stroke—a "new look" that, as opposed to the austere looks of the 1930s, made perfect sense.

New Look made Dior's name. His life came to a tragic, early end with his death at the age of 52 in 1957. But the look he created will always be remembered.

Coco Chanel poses in her salon in January 1962. Perhaps more than any other designer, Chanel influenced women's fashion and lifestyle.

elegant 1960s evening dresses of black chiffon or tubes of white sequins, a woman could be confident that her Chanel suit or dress would be as stylish the day she bought it as it would be one year later. It was in the details, the material, the cut, and the way it fit and flattered the woman wearing it that made it her own. And, working just as she had 40 years earlier, it was, for Chanel, a labor of love.

Writer Edmonde Charles-Roux, in his book *Chanel and Her World*, described the working process of the 80-year-old Chanel.

Again and again Chanel undid a jacket, cutting the stitches of an armhole, which she would then redo right on the mannequin, using pins to reposition it point by point, all stuck in with an almost demonic thrust. All the while she remained resolutely indifferent to everything but the creative process, a process that was slowly leading toward perfection. Her face tense, Coco scrutinized the work and, spotting a suspected bulge, seized upon the defect with fingers like talons. She would smooth and shape the material, because the flaw had to be eliminated. Finally satisfied, she would sit down, all but fainting with exhaustion . . . Then on to the next fitting.

Her life was her work, and her work was her life. Indeed, in the last years of her life, with many of her friends already deceased, Chanel's life was a lonely one. At the end, work was really all she had. Nothing could stop her. She suffered a small stroke in early 1970 that paralyzed her right arm. At the age of 87, she endured three months of physical therapy to regain the use of her hand. Without the use of her right arm, her career would be over, and to Chanel, that was just not acceptable.

On August 5, 1970, Chanel presented her spring 1971 collection. Fashion that year covered a wide range of styles—everything from maxi skirts (skirts that reached down to the ankles) to Japanese influences to tweeds to Hollywood glamour. But it was classic Chanel that was the big hit. The spring collection would be the last showing of her designs that she would attend.

On January 10, 1971, Coco Chanel died in her room at the Ritz. She was buried in Lausanne, Switzerland. Her last collection was shown on January 25 of that year, in a show presided over by French first lady Claude Pompidou. What was shown was classic Chanel: a pale tweed suit, sharply tailored suits, tunics, soft dresses, pleated skirts, and, at the end, the three white evening dresses that traditionally ended a Chanel fashion show. After it was over, the packed audience burst into wild applause, taking quick glances at Chanel's famous staircase, as though hoping that by their applause the legendary figure of Chanel could make one final appearance.

ELEMENTS OF STYLE

I wonder why I embarked on this profession, and why I'm thought of as a revolutionary figure? It was not in order to create what I liked, but rather so as to make what I disliked unfashionable. I have used my talent like an explosive. I have an eminently critical mind, and my eye too. "I have very certain dislikes," as Jules Renard said. All that I had seen bored me, I needed to cleanse my memory, to clear from my mind everything that I remembered. And I also needed to improve on what I had done and improve on what others were producing. I have been Fate's tool in a necessary cleansing process.

—*from* Chanel and Her World: Friends, Fashion, and Fame
by Edmonde Charles-Roux

LEGACY

Today, fashions have changed and the House of Chanel is run by others (although still controlled by the Wertheimer family), but the influence of Gabrielle Chanel is as strong today as it has ever been. Her biographer, Axel Madsen, summed up her achievement:

> The timeless appeal of Gabrielle Bonheur Chanel reigns supreme. The Chanel look is everywhere, canonized and copied with more fervor than ever before. Fashionable without being forward, the Chanel suit achieved new currency and appropriateness, a look that was rich, refined and, above all, dressed. Women's clothing based on gentlemanly elements, suits with jackets that fit like sweaters, masses of bogus jewelry replacing the demure real stuff, little black dresses, crisp white shirts, gold buttons, pleated skirts, navy jackets, quilted bags, and the black-tipped sling-back shoes are staples in the wardrobes of professional women.

It is an altogether remarkable achievement. The daughter of an itinerant merchant, the woman who in her later years tried to hide the truth about her childhood, the abandoned girl raised by nuns, went on to become one of the greatest influences on women's fashion in history. By liberating women from the fashion restraints of the past, by making it clear that casual clothes can also be elegant, by designing clothing that was meant to move with the woman, she changed the way women dressed, and thought of themselves, forever.

Chronology

1883	AUGUST 19 Gabrielle Chanel is born in Saumur, France.
1895	Jeanne Devolle Chanel, Gabrielle's mother, dies in February. Her father, Albert Chanel, disappears, so Gabrielle spends the next six years at the Aubazine orphanage run by the sisters of the Congregation of the Sacred Heart of Mary.
1901	Enters the Notre Dame finishing school.
1904	Gets her first job as a shopgirl and seamstress at the House of Grampayre.

TIMELINE

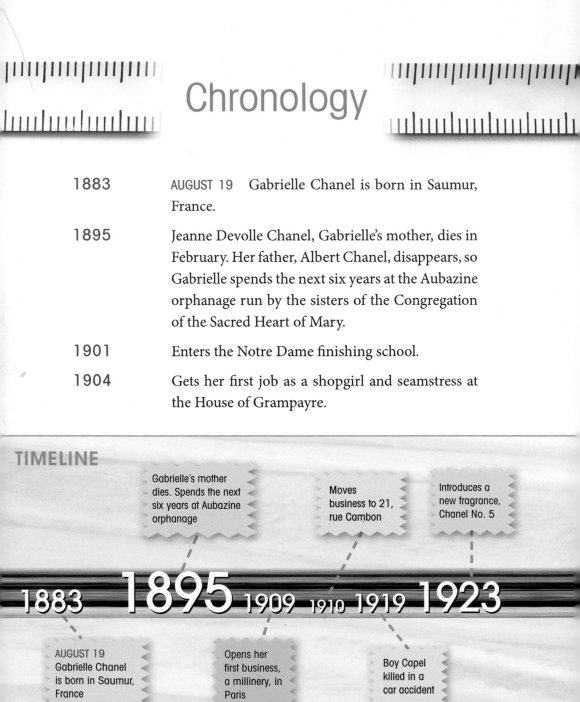

Gabrielle's mother dies. Spends the next six years at Aubazine orphanage

Moves business to 21, rue Cambon

Introduces a new fragrance, Chanel No. 5

1883 **1895** 1909 1910 1919 **1923**

AUGUST 19 Gabrielle Chanel is born in Saumur, France

Opens her first business, a millinery, in Paris

Boy Capel killed in a car accident

1906–1909	Lives at Royallieu with Étienne Balsan.
1909	Leaves Balsan for Arthur "Boy" Capel; opens her first business, a millinery, in Paris.
1910	Moves business to 21, rue Cambon.
1913	Opens a boutique in Deauville that becomes a huge success selling her line of women's sportswear, the first of its kind.
1915	Opens a boutique in Biarritz.
1919	Boy Capel killed in a car accident.
1923	Introduces a new fragrance, Chanel No. 5, which will become the world's best-known and best-selling perfume.
1924	Begins relationship with Hugh Richard Arthur Grosvenor, Duke of Westminster, known to his friends as Bender.

Begins relationship with Hugh Richard Arthur Grosvenor, Duke of Westminster

With the outbreak of World War II, closes the House of Chanel

Arrested and questioned about her wartime activities

Gabrielle Chanel dies at the age of 87

1924 1925 **1926** **1939** 1944 1954 **1971**

Introduces what becomes known as the classic Chanel suit

Introduces the "little black dress"

At the age of 70, Chanel stages her comeback

1925	Introduces what becomes known as the classic Chanel suit.
1926	Introduces the much-praised and much-copied "little black dress," which quickly becomes a staple of women's wardrobes around the world.
1930	Bender marries Loelia Mary Ponsonby.
1933	Chanel travels to the United States to explore the possibility of designing for films.
1939	With the outbreak of World War II, closes the House of Chanel.
1940	After briefly evacuating the city, Chanel returns to a Paris occupied by Germans. She moves back in to L'hôtel Ritz (the Hotel Ritz) for the duration of the war, and begins a relationship with Hans Gunther von Dincklage, a German officer and probable spy.
1943	At the behest of the Germans, Chanel travels to Madrid on a peace mission, hoping but failing to meet with her old friend, British prime minister Winston Churchill.
1944	After Paris is liberated from the Nazis, Chanel is arrested and questioned about her wartime activities, but is quickly released.
1946–1953	Chanel lives in quiet exile in Switzerland.
1954	At the age of 70, Chanel stages her comeback. After disastrous early reviews from the French and British press, her return is deemed a triumph by Americans and becomes a success.
1971	Gabrielle Chanel dies at the age of 87 in her room at L'hôtel Ritz.

Glossary

Belle Époque   A period of artistic and social refinement, especially in France at the beginning of the twentieth century.

boater   A stiff straw hat with a flat crown.

bodice   The part of the dress above the waist.

cardigan jacket   A collarless knitted sweater or jacket that opens down the front.

dowry   The money or property a wife brings to her husband at marriage.

impresario   A manger or producer of public entertainments, including theater, music, and dance.

jersey   A soft, elastic, knitted cloth.

New Look   A style of women's clothing designed by Christian Dior in 1947, which typically involved a tight bodice, narrow waist, and a flowing, pleated skirt.

paradox   A statement that contradicts itself.

Popular Front   A coalition of left-wing parties united against fascism.

silhouette   The shape that clothing and undergarments give.

Slavic   Relating to Slavic or Russian culture.

sportswear   Clothing worn for sport or casual wear.

 # Bibliography

Charles-Roux, Edmonde. *Chanel and Her World: Friends, Fashion, and Fame.* New York: Vendome Press, 2005.

De La Haye, Amy, and Shelley Tobin. *Chanel: The Couturiere at Work.* Woodstock, N.Y.: Overlook Press, 1996.

Madsen, Axel. *Chanel: A Woman of Her Own.* New York: Holt Paperbacks, 1991.

Morand, Paul. *The Allure of Chanel.* London: Pushkin Press, 2008.

 # Further Resources

Aveline, Françoise. *Chanel Perfume*. New York: Assouline, 2005.

Breward, Christopher. *Fashion* (Oxford History of Art). New York: Oxford University Press U.S.A., 2003.

Buxbaum, Gerda. *Icons of Fashion: The 20th Century*. Munich; New York: Prestel Publishing, 2005.

Koda, Harold, Andres Bolton, Rhonda Garelick, and Karl Lagerfeld. *Chanel*. New York: Metropolitan Museum of Art, 2005.

Richards, Melissa. *Chanel: Key Collections*. New York: Welcome Rain Publishers, 2000.

Watson, Linda. *20th Century Fashion: 100 Years of Style by Decade and Designer, in Association with Vogue*. Buffalo, New York: Firefly Books, 2004.

Picture Credits

Index

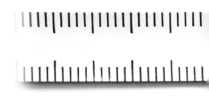

About the Author

DENNIS ABRAMS is the author of many books for Chelsea House, including biographies of Hillary Rodham Clinton, H.G. Wells, Rachael Ray, Xerxes, Albert Pujols, Georgia O'Keefe, and Nicolas Sarkozy. He attended Antioch College, where he majored in English and communications. A voracious reader since the age of three, Dennis lives in Houston with his partner of 21 years as well as three cats and a dog, Junie B.